5-MINUTE PLAYS

THE APPLAUSE ACTING SERIES

THE APPLAUSE ACTING SERIES

5-MINUTE PLAYS

EDITED BY

LAWRENCE HARBISON

APPLAUSE
THEATRE & CINEMA BOOKS
AN IMPRINT OF HAL LEONARD LLC

Published in 2017 by Applause Theatre & Cinema Books

An Imprint of Hal Leonard LLC
7777 West Bluemound Road
Milwaukee, WI 53213

Trade Book Division Editorial Offices
33 Plymouth St., Montclair, NJ 07042

Printed in the United States of America

Book design by Lynn Bergesen, UB Communications

Library of Congress Cataloging-in-Publication Data is available upon request.

ISBN 978-1-4950-6924-6

www.applausebooks.com

CONTENTS

INTRODUCTION

At the time that Actors Theatre of Louisville began commissioning 10-minute plays for use by their apprentice company, there was no such idea of the 10-minute play as a viable form. When I got the idea, as Editor at Samuel French, to publish an anthology of ATL's plays, I thought that maybe students might find them of use for class. Never in my wildest imaginings did I anticipate the boom in 10-minute-play festivals all over the world, which all came about because for the first time plays of this length were now readily available. What is a "5-minute" play? The glib answer, which happens to be true, is that it's a full-length play that runs about 5 minutes.

Now, I am starting to see 5-minute-play festivals cropping up. Clearly, there is a burgeoning market for plays of this length, which is why Applause asked me to do two volumes of these plays—one for adults, one for teens.

This volume is the one for adults. Some plays are comic (laughs); some are dramatic (no laughs). Some are realistic in style, some more unconventional. Their length also makes them perfect for scene work in class. A few of the plays are by playwrights who have established quite a reputation with their full-length plays, such as Don Nigro, Lee Blessing, Y York, and Sheila Callaghan; but most are by what I call exciting up-and-comers, such as Nicole Pandolfo, Merridith Allen, Andrew Biss, Adam Kraar, Stephanie Hutchinson, Judy Klass, John McKinney, and Scott C. Sickles (all of whom I have included in the annual 10-minute play anthologies I edit); and Graham Techler, Eric Grant, Deanna Alisa Ableser, Kerri Kochanski, Lisa Bruna, and Grace Trotta.

What makes a "good" 5-minute play? First and foremost, let's face it, I have to like it; but I also think it will interest people who want to produce plays of this length.

I hope you like the plays in this book as much as I did.

Lawrence Harbison

THE AGENT

Lewis Gardner

First performed at Woodstock Renaissance Faire, Woodstock, New York, July 1997, by the Woodstock Theater Cooperative.

CHARACTERS

RODOLFO: An agent, 30s to 50s.
MARCO: A boy soprano, 12.
GRAZIELLA: A young woman, 12–13.

(*Any of these characters can be played by adult women.* RODOLFO *would become* RAFAELLA.)

TIME

The 1700s.

SETTING

Italy. Backstage at a cathedral.

(RODOLFO *is discussing business with* MARCO.)

RODOLFO   Kid, that was a fantastic "Gloria." Knocked my pantaloons off. Not to mention the Agnus Dei. That was the best singing I've heard since I left Rome last week.

MARCO   Thank you, signor.

RODOLFO   Been singing long?

MARCO   Since I was a child. Of course, I'm still only twelve.

RODOLFO   That's good. That's funny.

MARCO   Excuse me, signor. Thank you for the compliments, but who are you? I'm in a bit of a hurry—I'm joining my family to view a hanging in front of the cathedral.

RODOLFO   Oh, of course. Forgive my importunity. Here's my card.

MARCO   (*Reading.*) "Rodolfo Caputo, Talent Representative, The Vatican." Oh, do you work for the Pope?

RODOLFO   The Holy Father himself. We're very good personal friends.

MARCO   Pleased to meet you, signor.

RODOLFO   Hey, I'm tickled pink that I found you, kid. To cut to the chase, we've been looking all over Europe. We need someone for the soprano solo in a new motet by Palestrina.

MARCO   I like Palestrina's motets.

RODOLFO   This one has a good beat, and you can pray to it.—Stick with me, kid, and I can guarantee a great career. You'll be celebrated all over the continent, you'll have the finest wine, the adoration of huge crowds, sweetmeats, velvet doublets, shoes by this new bootmaker, Gucci.

MARCO   Sounds good. Hmmm. Is there any kind of a catch? I suppose you collect a commission.

RODOLFO   Ten percent. Standard for the business. But I'm in this racket because of my love of beautiful music. For the glory of God, as a matter of fact.

MARCO   And that's it? All I give up is ten percent?

RODOLFO   Not exactly. You'll also have to make a little . . . sacrifice.

MARCO   I'm willing to work hard. I'll study, I'll put in long hours. I could give up bocce, I suppose. Of course, I can't guarantee my voice won't change. It happened to Giorgio last month—his voice cracked in the middle of a Sanctus. The Cardinal busted a gut!

(*Laughs.*)

RODOLFO   Well, in fact, you have hit the crux of the matter on the nail. A little sacrifice . . . ?

MARCO   Oh.

(*His expressions go through a wide range of processing—including looking down to his groin area. He realizes. He discreetly covers himself with his cap.*)

I don't think my father would approve of that. . . .

RODOLFO I can make him a generous offer. A good sum as soon as he signs the contract. Let's go and see him now.

MARCO Why don't you talk to Orlando, signor? Orlando with the carbuncle on his nose? He'll do anything for a career.

RODOLFO Kid—think about it: I can get your picture in *L'Osservatore Romano*.

MARCO Gossip section?—*Front page . . . ?*

RODOLFO It's a distinct possibility.

MARCO Can we make a deal on the royalties?

RODOLFO I'll have my people talk to Palestrina's people—I'm sure we can work something out.

(*Noises off.*)

MARCO Hey—they're starting the hanging!

RODOLFO Wait a minute—can we shake on my proposal?

(GRAZIELLA, *a luscious wench and groupie, comes in.*)

GRAZIELLA Hello, Master Marco!

MARCO (*Delighted.*) Graziella! Bon giorno!

GRAZIELLA I heard you singing that Mater Dolorosa number. It was multo groovy.

MARCO (*Blushing.*) Gosh, thanks.

GRAZIELLA Are you going to the execution? My great-uncle, the Duke of Cappuccino-Grande, has a window overlooking the gallows. We can be alone. . . .

MARCO You bet! Got any sweetmeats?

(*She smiles and winks.*)

GRAZIELLA What do you think?

MARCO (*To* RODOLFO.) So long, signore.

RODOLFO But the contract—?

MARCO Ask Orlando!

RODOLFO What about the career? Don't you want a career?

MARCO Yeah, I do—I want to be a great baritone!

(*He and* GRAZIELLA *rush off.*)

RODOLFO Damn kids nowadays—no respect for art.

 END OF PLAY

AMAZEMENT AND JELLY

Susan Goodell

CHARACTERS

DR. CUSTER: Formal, overconfident man, 30s or older.

DR. CLEM: Dr. Custer's intimidated, placating associate, late 20s or older.

SETTING

A small auditorium where an important medical presentation is soon to take place.

NOTE

Just fake your way through the pronunciations.

(*At rise:* DR. WILLIAM CUSTER *and* DR. ROBERT CLEM *are on an empty stage, preparing for an important medical presentation taking place within the next hour. The audience is soon to arrive.* DR. CUSTER *is scurrying to arrange PAPERS, VISUAL AIDS, and a LARGE JAR OF A PRODUCT.* DR. CLEM *is trying to help.*)

DR. CUSTER   (*Harried.*) What time is it?

DR. CLEM   45 minutes.

DR. CUSTER   Don't tell me that.

DR. CLEM   But you . . .

DR. CUSTER   Never mind. We're ready for this. We are ready. (*Picks up report and becomes alarmed.*) What's this on the front page?

DR. CLEM   What? Where?

DR. CUSTER   (*Disapproving.*) Carrageenan right there?

DR. CLEM   That's what you told me to put.

DR. CUSTER   I never would tell you Carrageenan. I told you Palmitate.

DR. CLEM   No you didn't. It's clearly in your notes

DR. CUSTER   Didn't you understand that? That's a typo.

DR. CLEM   Dr. Custer, I'm starting to wonder . . .

DR. CUSTER   I don't like it when you wonder.

DR. CLEM   I just think . . .

DR. CUSTER   I will not postpone. That's what you were going to say, wasn't it?

DR. CLEM   But Doctor . . .

DR. CUSTER   Everyone wants to undermine me. You want to undermine me, and you're my most trusted colleague.

DR. CLEM   I'm trying to tell you.

DR. CUSTER   You do understand the prestige Flavonite M. will bestow upon us? What this will mean to our futures? This is going to be the most memorable hour of your life. Tell me how much you're anticipating this.

DR. CLEM   I am anticipating this.

DR. CUSTER   I hope that was sincere.

DR. CLEM   Doctor I'm with you. But people. Some people . . . you know how they're always skeptics.

DR. CUSTER   They're not skeptics. They're wishing it were them making the announcement today. Should I wear my lab jacket or a coat and tie?

DR. CLEM   Dr. Custer. As I go through our presentation there are parts of it that . . .

DR. CUSTER   That are amazing.

DR. CLEM   That's true, Dr. Custer.

DR. CUSTER   Don't call this a new product. Call it the opening of a frontier.

DR. CLEM   Yes, Doctor. But we might have a few more typos in here.

Dr. Custer   Why do you say that?

Dr. Clem   Well, Dr. Filer's team for one . . .

Dr. Custer   Oh oh oh oh oh. You've been talking to Dr. Filer's team.

Dr. Clem   They contacted me after the first clinical trials.

Dr. Custer   And you talked to them?

Dr. Clem   They found some contradictions.

Dr. Custer   Well, so what.

Dr. Clem   They said they didn't believe anything in your tests actually.

Dr. Custer   They just didn't understand it. Did they?

Dr. Clem   It seems like they . . .

Dr. Custer   They didn't understand it.

Dr. Clem   OK.

Dr. Custer   Robert. Look at the calendar.

Dr. Clem   It's May 7.

Dr. Custer   Exactly. May 7. And I want you to remember May 7, because May 7th will be forever more remembered. The day that—Flavonite M—was first announced.

Dr. Clem   It's going to be quite a day.

Dr. Custer   You know the problem. People just can't believe in the product.

Dr. Clem   They don't believe the product at all.

Dr. Custer   They say we couldn't develop a treatment that offers weight loss, overcoming depression, curing shyness, dust mite immunity, and dry mouth therapy, one spoonful once a day. Well, we just did.

Dr. Clem   We'll have to prove it.

DR. CUSTER   Well, we have. Because our thinking is not limited like Dr. Filer's thinking. Dr. Filer's—team.

DR. CLEM   Dr. Custer? Did you hear that Dr. Filer's team actually did their own analysis of Flavonite M?

DR. CUSTER   Good for them.

DR. CLEM   Their results were . . .

DR. CUSTER   Leave it to Dr. Filer's team . . .

DR. CLEM   Their results were . . .

DR. CUSTER   Results. I doubt Dr. Filer's team has ever achieved such a thing as a result.

DR. CLEM   Their results were quite different than our results. In fact, they're claiming, in their own compositional analysis which they plan to announce after your announcement, that Flavonite M. is actually arachis hypogaea.

DR. CUSTER   Of course they got different results. Am I supposed to be surprised?

DR. CLEM   Dr. Custer. Arachis hypogaea is peanut butter.

END OF PLAY

THE AUTHOR'S AUTOPSY

Stacey Lane

The Author's Autopsy was first produced on June 1, 2013 by South Simcoe Theatre in Cookstown, Ontario, Canada. The director was Sandy Bishop. The artistic director was Christina Luck. The technical director was Drew Murdoch. The tech crew included Mark Hoffman, Jennifer Noel, and Amelie Larente. The cast was as follows:

DR. OWENS: Barb Canning
DR. SHIFFLET: Cheryl Studdy
CORPSE: Kevin Scharf

CHARACTERS

DR. OWENS: Chief forensic pathologist (male or female, any age)
DR. SHIFFLET: Resident (male or female, any age)

TIME

The present.

SETTING

An examination table in the autopsy suite of a morgue.

———————

(*At rise:* DR. OWENS *and* DR. SHIFFLET *stand over a corpse, tools at the ready.*)

DR. OWENS   If you need to vomit in this bucket, I won't think less of you.

DR. SHIFFLET   This may be my first autopsy, Doctor, but I assure you I come highly trained.

DR. OWENS   Nothing you read in books can prepare you for this. Shall we begin with the standard Y incision of the cavity or the coronal incision of the scalp?

DR. SHIFFLET   The brain, if you don't mind.

DR. OWENS   Do the honors.

(DR. SHIFFLET *makes the incision to the head.*)

DR. SHIFFLET   Hmmmm. Uh . . .

DR. OWENS   This man was an artist, an author.

DR. SHIFFLET   Awh, that accounts for the abnormalities.

DR. OWENS   Begin your examination.

(DR. SHIFFLET *pulls out a small yellow note.*)

DR. OWENS   What did you find?

DR. SHIFFLET   Some sappy sentiments about a sunset.

DR. OWENS   Pass me the puke pail.

DR. SHIFFLET   Pardon?

DR. OWENS   My apologies. But when you've seen as many of these as I have . . .

(DR. OWENS *pulls out hundreds upon hundreds of notes.* DR. SHIFFLET *follows suit.*)

DR. OWENS   Plotlines, premises, possible titles, possible pen names, character descriptions, witty observations about life, rants on religion, questioning of political ideals, unresolved father issues, inkling of genius, overheard conversations at restaurants, clever sayings stolen from friends—

DR. SHIFFLET   (*Studying a note.*) Hmmmm . . .

DR. OWENS   Discover something noteworthy?

DR. SHIFFLET   An idea for a novel.

DR. OWENS   Yes, yes. There are plenty of those in here.

DR. SHIFFLET   But this one's not bad. I mean I'd read that book.

DR. OWENS   Yes. Well, you'll never get the chance now.
   (DR. OWENS *measures the notes on a scale and writes on the chart.*)
   For this much material, the volume of work is surprisingly low.

DR. SHIFFLET   So that's what killed him then. All those jumbled thoughts wrapped in angst and discontent crashing against each other in a quest for ultimately unattainable fulfillment.

DR. OWENS   No. No. That's the norm for these creative types. When there's nothing up there, that's when there's cause for concern. Shall we move on to the standard Y incision?

DR. SHIFFLET   Yes, Doctor.

(DR. SHIFFLET *makes the incision to the body.*)

DR. OWENS   My! My! I've never seen bowel blockage of this magnitude.

(*Pulling out gobs and gobs of crumpled up notebook paper and typed pages.*)

Discarded drafts, abandoned books, neglected novels, rejected rewrites . . .

DR. SHIFFLET   What a waste!

DR. OWENS   Aha. There it is. The cause of death.

(*Pulls out a nicely bound book.*)

DR. SHIFFLET   (*Reading title.*) "My Magnum Opus."

DR. OWENS   It was pressing on his heart.

DR. SHIFFLET   (*Opening book.*) It's blank.

(*Blackout*)

END OF PLAY

BAGGAGE GAME

Lynne Bolen

Baggage Game was first produced at the Empire Theatre in December 2010, directed by Lynne Bolen, and starred Lynne Bolen and John Bolen.

CHARACTERS

CAROL: 50s–60s, female
TIM: 50s–60s, male

TIME

Early November, present.

SETTING

Furniture section of a department store. A sofa is center stage.

———————————

(*At rise:* CAROL *pulls* TIM *over to the sofa.*)

CAROL   This looks like a good one!

TIM   (*Plopping onto the sofa.*) Gotta see how it rides.

CAROL   Tim, you're not test driving a car.

TIM   Sit down Carol. See how it fits.

CAROL   What style do you like?

TIM   I dunno, a couch is a couch is a couch . . .

CAROL   (*Interjects.*) Sofa.

TIM   "Couch," Carol. "Sofa" is for sissies.

CAROL   I doubt the owners of Sofa City or Sofa King would agree
with you.

TIM   The game show is *Couch Potatoes*, not sofa potatoes.

CAROL   Well, you're clearly the expert there. You spend countless
hours on the sofa watching your game shows on TV.

TIM   I knew this was a bad idea. We're arguing over what to call a
couch, let alone picking one.

CAROL   We have to replace the sofa. It's old, lumpy, covered in dog
hair, and the evil cat has shredded it.

TIM It's comfortable.

CAROL Take a look at the tag. How much does it cost?

TIM Come on down, Carol, "the price is right"!

CAROL Price isn't everything. We have to consider color, style, and whether there is a matching loveseat. There you go, sofa and loveseat. Nobody ever says couch and loveseat.

TIM I never say loveseat.

CAROL What do you think of the style? It will look good with the buffet.

TIM Buffet? You're planning to serve food on the couch?

CAROL The buffet, where the china is stored. The hutch?

TIM Oh, you mean the sideboard.

CAROL Let's focus on the sofa. Shall we buy it?

TIM I suppose it's okay, as long as it doesn't "break the bank."

CAROL You're addicted to game shows. What do you think?

TIM "I've got a secret." I really don't think we need a new one.

CAROL We've discussed this. It's our first Thanksgiving together, and you want a big family gathering. I can't have everyone seeing that disgraceful sofa.

TIM You're getting too wound up over this Thanksgiving dinner. To tell the truth, nobody cares about the couch. They're only interested in the bountiful buffet of turkey, cornbread stuffing, giblet gravy, green bean casserole, and lime Jell-O.

CAROL Whoa there, cowboy, no bellying up to a buffet. The Thanksgiving feast is a sit-down dinner with china, crystal, and silver.

TIM You're overdoing things. The grandkids are too young. They'll make a mess at the table.

CAROL   And there will be Mrs. Cubbison's dressing, normal gravy, creamed corn, and no yucky Jell-O made out of horses' hooves.

TIM   We've always had the same menu and if you change things up, there'll be a family feud.

CAROL   Things can never be the same. It's a losing situation from the get-go.

TIM   You sound negative. I thought you wanted to do this.

CAROL   Tim, *you* want to do this.

TIM   But what about you? "Truth or consequences."

CAROL   I agreed because I wanted you to be happy, but . . . to be honest . . . I think it would be a huge mistake.

TIM   I can't believe this. Everyone wants to have Thanksgiving dinner at the house.

CAROL   Tim, you have this idealistic image in your head of recreating the big family Thanksgiving, but I seriously doubt your kids want it. It can never be the same without their mother.

TIM   And your kids. It's the perfect opportunity to blend the family.

CAROL   They're all adults and probably don't want to be blended. I think they'd rather spend Thanksgiving with their father.

TIM   I want my kids to hold onto their memories.

CAROL   Your kids, Tim, or you?

TIM   We were married for thirty-one years, a lifetime of memories.

CAROL   (*Emotionally.*) I shouldn't have moved into your home. I know it's only temporary until we can sell it and buy our own house together, but everywhere I turn, she's there. You put her high on a pedestal and cling to your memories. Are you still in love with her?

TIM   (*Flatly.*) She's dead.

CAROL   You can't deny that you're still in love with her memory.

TIM   (*Hurt and angry.*) It's easy for you. You're divorced. You didn't lose someone you love.

CAROL   I did lose someone I love! We were high school sweethearts, together for thirty years, and I mourn the death of our marriage and our family. I still love Greg. I've known him longer than I have known anyone, and he is my children's father.

TIM   I'm sorry. It's complicated.

CAROL   Everyone said that we shouldn't have rushed into marriage. Your kids, my kids, our friends. They said it was a rebound relationship for me, divorced only a year. They said it was way too soon for you, just ten months since Angie passed. You're still grieving.

TIM   I had been grieving for the five years since she got sick. It was time for me start living again.

CAROL   I know it was tough. You couldn't just go out to the ball game or the movies.

TIM   So I became a couch potato.

CAROL   (*Teasingly slugging* TIM.) Sofa slug.

TIM   I have never confessed this to anyone, but when it was over, I felt . . . relieved.

CAROL   That's normal. The burden was lifted. I felt relieved when my marriage was over.

TIM   Didn't you just say you still love Greg?

CAROL   I love him, but I am not in love with him. I'm in love with you.

TIM   When I met you, I began to live again.

CAROL   A new life began for me, too.

TIM   So, you really don't want to do the big family Thanksgiving dinner?

CAROL   Nobody does.

TIM   Carol, "let's make a deal." We won't do Thanksgiving at the house, and we won't buy a new couch.

CAROL   (*Doing the beauty pageant wave.*) We'll go out to a restaurant for Thanksgiving, and I'll be "queen for a day."

TIM   And we'll invite all of our kids and their spouses and the grandkids to join us, if they'd like. "Deal or no deal."

(TIM *extends his hand,* CAROL *firmly shakes it. Then* TIM *gently kisses* CAROL's *hand, and* CAROL *curtsies.*)

CAROL   It's funny that no salesperson has come by.

TIM   They probably saw us and hid. I would have. Can we go home now?

CAROL   Not yet. That "deal or no deal" gave me an idea. Let's go over to the luggage department.

TIM   You need a new briefcase?

CAROL   No, we need luggage.

TIM   My luggage is fine.

CAROL   If we buy a matching set of luggage, we can get rid of the baggage from the past.

TIM   I see the game you're playing. Okay, matching luggage, as long as they have four wheels.

CAROL   Let me guess. "Wheels of fortune?"

TIM   No, with my back, bags are challenging! (*Beat.*) You know, Carol, we don't need new luggage at all. Let's just park our old baggage outside and slam the door shut.

CAROL   It's a deal. We'll start anew.

TIM   Thank goodness. For a while there, I was afraid our marriage was in "jeopardy."

CAROL It's just the "newlywed game."

TIM Let's go home and snuggle in the sofa bed.

CAROL Aha, not the couch bed?

(TIM *and* CAROL *exit, hand in hand.*)

END OF PLAY

BOOKS DON'T KILL PEOPLE

Vanessa David

Books Don't Kill People was originally produced by Another Country Productions for SLAMBoston in March of 2006.

Original cast

DAD: Jordan Harrison

MOM: Lyralen Kaye

SUZIE: Emily Evans

BOBBY: Shaun Mitchell

CHARACTERS

DAD: Head of the household, breadwinner/deer killer.

WIFE: Fulfilling her role and duties while retaining a certain naturalism. Underneath it all, she is a realist.

SUZIE: Daughter. A realist like her Mother. She is more willing to stand up to her father.

BOBBY: The "good" son. Going through life with his headphones on.

SETTING

The set is that of an all-American, white family. Breakfast room, a table for four. A place to hang coats, school bags.

———————

(*At rise:* DAD *is seated at table eating his breakfast.*)

DAD   (*To audience.*) Hello. I am Neanderthal man. I am a hunter and a capitalist. I work all day to feed my family. I commute. My wife feeds me every morning to fuel my body for the commute, the most draining ritual known to Capitalist Neanderthal Man.

WIFE   (*Entering with eggs.*) More eggs, dear?

DAD   My wife. She is a gatherer. When she's not taking the kids somewhere.

WIFE   (*Listing to herself; she knows he won't hear.*) Gatherer, laundress, chef, baker, housekeeper, slave—

DAD   Dear, why don't you check on the kids.

WIFE   (*Exiting, aside to audience.*) White guilt.

DAD   Dear?

WIFE   (*To him as she exits.*) I'm going.

DAD   I like my home clean, controlled. I praise parental controls, warning labels on music and video games. I shun newspaper publications, magazines. My wife will never hear the term "chick-lit." (*To a man in the audience.*) That's literature for women. I didn't know either; I had to ask the director. I keep my interaction with so called "art" to a minimum. People just don't paint like Rockwell anymore.

SUZIE   (*Enters with a book behind her.*) Hi, Dad.

DAD   Mornin', Suzie. Ready for your first day of school?

SUZIE   Sure. (*Trying to put the book in her bag without him seeing.*)

DAD   What have you got there?

SUZIE   A book.

DAD   A book? What kind of book?

SUZIE   It's nothing.

DAD   Let me see it. (*Like it's heroin.*) Where did you get this?!

SUZIE   Dad, calm down. It's just a book.

DAD   *Love Makes a Family*! Who sold you these lies?

SUZIE   Dad, it's just a book. You know, knowledge is power. Information leads to understanding, creating empathy . . . (*Indicating the audience, and he IS an actor.*) c'mon it's kinda method, Dad. You should know this . . .

DAD   (*Now he wants to stay in the scene.*) Don't go changing the subject on me, young lady. Where did you get this?

SUZIE   I bought it for a friend.

DAD   A friend?

WIFE   (*Enters, followed by* BOBBY.) What's going on?

DAD   She was taking a book to school!

BOBBY   What's the world coming to?

DAD   *Love Makes a Family*. (*He hands to book to* WIFE; *she starts to read through it.*)

BOBBY   What a loser!

SUZIE   Shut up, Bobby!

DAD   What are you taking to school Bobby?

BOBBY   My video game. *Carjacking and Crack Whore Whacking.*

DAD   That's my boy! (*To audience.*) You may wonder how I can justify that—

SUZIE   Dad, this is not a good time to break the fourth wall!

DAD   I'm talking to the audience.

WIFE   She's right, dear. You did your "I'm Neanderthal Man" presentational thing already. Now it's family time. (*She goes back to reading.*)

DAD   I don't want her reading that book. I don't want anyone accepting anyone for who they are and how they think God made them. Tolerance is for the weak! You start accepting everyone and who knows what will happen!?

BOBBY   Ha, ha—accepting everyone! Good one Suzie. Dad, can I take your gun to school?

DAD   Sure, Son.

(BOBBY *puts on his stereo headphones and gets the gun and puts it in his bag. He then gets lost in his video game.* SUZIE *speaks over the action.*)

SUZIE   I don't believe this. You're letting him take a gun to school and I can't take a book called *Love Makes a Family*?! And you can't even come up with a logical reason why!

DAD   Because you can't go around saying loves makes a family, it's not right . . . it's—it's—

SUZIE   You can't even think of a reason.

DAD   It's not me—it's the playwright! (*Under his breath.*) Theater liberals.

SUZIE   Stop blaming others, Dad. What's wrong with "love makes a family?" NOTHING!

DAD   You can't say that. That's not the way it's supposed to be.

WIFE   YOU don't know that, dear!

(*EVERYONE STOPS for a moment, except* BOBBY, *who's engrossed in his game.*)

DAD   What?

WIFE   You don't know that, dear. You can't possibly know that.

DAD   I am Capitalist Neanderthal Man.

WIFE   CUT THE CRAP AND JUST BE REAL FOR A MINUTE! (*Beat. This isn't a play anymore.*) These are just our roles. When we leave here, we're individuals. And whatever we do as those individuals, whatever role we assume—OUTSIDE of here—doesn't affect you. So why do you care? Why should you care? I'll tell you what—you shouldn't. Now. Back to acting. (*Beat. It's now a melodrama, musical theatre without music. They all speak with exaggerated southern accents.*) STOP worrying about that book, damnit, and stop your son before he goes to school with that goddamn gun!

DAD   Why, you're right, Stella. What was I thinking?

SUZIE   Oh, Pa. I knew you'd see the light.

(DAD *starts to cross to* BOBBY. BOBBY, *still engrossed in his game, looks up to see something horrifying. Something they didn't rehearse.*)

BOBBY   Wait a minute. What? Were there rewrites? I don't remember this moment. Shit.

DAD   Son, I love you too much to let you ruin your life by taking that gun to school. Give me the gun, Son.

BOBBY   Aww, Daaaad.

WIFE   I knew you'd do the right thing, Jim.

DAD   Son, you can't go bringin' a loaded gun to school. What would people think?

SUZIE   Tell him Pa. Guns kill people.

DAD   No Suzie, guns don't kill people, people kill people (*To audience in his normal voice.*) But books, folks, books are something different altogether. Never underestimate the power of a good book. You just may discover for yourself, that love truly does make a family.

(*Blackout*)

END OF PLAY

CARBON-BASED LIFE FORM SEEKS SIMILAR

Andrew Biss

The original version of *Carbon-Based Life Form Seeks Similar* was first produced by the Independent Theatre Collective as part of its StoFest One-Act Play Festival in 2010, in Wheeling, West Virginia. The play was directed by Melody Meadows.

The play was subsequently produced by the Curan Repertory Company as part of its Notes from the Underground Festival in 2011 at the American Theatre of Actors, New York, New York. Directed by Nicole Allen and performed by Darlene McCullough and Lee Soloman.

CHARACTERS

MR. LOVEWORTH: The owner of a dating agency. Age open.
LESLIE: A woman looking to date again. Age open.

TIME

The present.

SETTING

The Happy Endings Dating Agency.

(*At rise:* MR. LOVEWORTH *is found seated behind his desk, scribbling notes into a book. Presently, there is a knock at the door. Upon opening it he discovers* LESLIE.)

MR. LOVEWORTH   You must be Leslie.

LESLIE   Yes. And you must be Mr. Loveworth.

MR. LOVEWORTH   Right again.

LESLIE   Sorry?

MR. LOVEWORTH   Do come in.

LESLIE   Thank you.

MR. LOVEWORTH   Firstly, let me say welcome to the Happy Endings Dating Agency—where love isn't just a dream, it's a calculated decision.

LESLIE   Thank you.

MR. LOVEWORTH   Do take a seat.

LESLIE   You're a little different than I imagined.

MR. LOVEWORTH   How so?

LESLIE   I don't know. Something about your voice—I imagined you taller.

MR. LOVEWORTH   I have a tall voice?

LESLIE   Well, no, I . . .

MR. LOVEWORTH   So, what brings you to our humble, and some might say, old fashioned little establishment?

LESLIE   Well, boredom, I suppose. Boredom with my non-existent love life. It's like there's a void inside of me that needs filling. I admit I did try a few of the online agencies first, but it all felt so anonymous and . . . well, cold, really.

MR. LOVEWORTH   You don't have to explain to me, Leslie. We here at Happy Endings are quite aware that when it comes to love, there's no substitute for the personal touch. Now, there's absolutely no reason to lose heart—you simply need to pay a little mind to how others perceive you.

LESLIE   But . . . I don't know how to be anything other than who I am.

MR. LOVEWORTH   And therein lies the problem.

LESLIE   But this is it—this is me.

MR. LOVEWORTH   But it's not enough. It's not enough to just be in this day and age.

LESLIE   Why ever not?

MR. LOVEWORTH   Look, Leslie, I'm trying to help you achieve your goals, but if I'm to do so, you're going to have to confront some uncomfortable truths. Now, in prehistoric times, things were much more straightforward. You could simply wrap yourself in a pelt, grunt a few times at your heart's desire, and live happily ever after. These days things are a little more complicated. Every aspect of your being has to be cultivated and contrived. Nothing can be left to chance. The way you dress, the way you walk, the way you smile, the way you talk, all of it has to be manufactured with absolute precision in order to create the *real* you—the one that closes the deal. Then and only then will you have become something truly viable in today's fickle and uncertain market.

(*Pause.*)

LESLIE   Can't someone just love me for who I am?

MR. LOVEWORTH   But if you don't know who you are—what's to love?

(*Beat.*)

LESLIE   The question marks?

MR. LOVEWORTH   Let me put it this way. Let's say I send you out to meet with a very nice gentleman who you find yourself very attracted to, and the next evening you anxiously await his call. He, meanwhile, that very same evening, is enjoying cocktails with friends who are all eager to hear the outcome of his first date, and to whom he relays any one of the following: "She redefined the word dull." "From the way she dressed I assumed she was manic depressive." "Her hair kept reminding me of my grandmother." "She was nice enough, but God, that annoying laugh!" Or perhaps, "In a million years I could *never* get used to that nose."

(*Beat.*)

Do you see what I mean?

LESLIE   (*Overwhelmed.*) I . . . it's . . . it's all too much. I . . . can't do it.

MR. LOVEWORTH   Incidentally, *your* nose—have you considered surgery?

LESLIE   Oh, that's it. That is it! I've had it!

MR. LOVEWORTH   I was only going to suggest a slight—

LESLIE   This is ridiculous!

(*Standing.*)

I'm sorry, I've had enough.

MR. LOVEWORTH   I'm sorry?

LESLIE   I've had enough.

MR. LOVEWORTH   Look, let's not overreact. I'm here to help.

LESLIE   Yes . . . and you have. You really have.

MR. LOVEWORTH   Good. Now sit down and let's—

LESLIE   I'm leaving.

MR. LOVEWORTH   Now?

LESLIE   I should never have come.

MR. LOVEWORTH   What about love?

LESLIE   I've gone off it.

MR. LOVEWORTH   But you need it. Everyone does.

LESLIE   It's too much trouble.

MR. LOVEWORTH   But your boredom? Your void?

LESLIE   I'll fill it with something else.

MR. LOVEWORTH   A cat?

LESLIE   A catechism. I'll take the vows.

MR. LOVEWORTH   A nun?

LESLIE   I hear a calling.

MR. LOVEWORTH   I hear nothing.

LESLIE   Thanks for everything.

MR. LOVEWORTH   But don't you want—

LESLIE   Goodbye.

(LESLIE *exits.*)

MR. LOVEWORTH   . . . a happy ending?

(*Blackout.*)

END OF PLAY

CARVED-OUT LIGHT

Stephanie Hutchinson

Reading: August 1, 2010

Theatre Encino, Encino, California

LUCIDA: Marina Palmier
OBSCURA: Fay Gauthier
MAN'S VOICE (OFFSTAGE): Paul Cuneo
WOMAN'S VOICE (OFFSTAGE): Michelle DeLynn

Director: Lisa Soland

CHARACTERS

LUCIDA: (pronounced LOO'si-da), 30s–40s female, a beautiful opaque glass vase. SHE wears an outfit like a Fruit of the Loom character, with a round "vase" around her midsection. There is a clear stripe through the center, through which we can see an interior light. SHE is thankful.

OBSCURA: 20s–30s female, a beautiful opaque glass vase. SHE wears an outfit like a Fruit of the Loom character, with a round "vase" around her midsection. There is a clear stripe through the center, but SHE does not have an interior light. SHE is ungrateful and haughty.

MAN'S VOICE, OFFSTAGE
WOMAN'S VOICE, OFFSTAGE

TIME

The present.

SETTING

An art gallery.

NOTE

Carved-Out Light was inspired by the glasswork of Lino Tagliapietra. The lighting effect can be achieved by battery-powered candles.

––––––––––––––

(*At rise:* LUCIDA *is sitting on a shelf, humming "Oh What a Beautiful Morning" from* Oklahoma.)

(OBSCURA *enters and sits next to* LUCIDA.)

LUCIDA   (*Friendly.*) Good morning!

OBSCURA   (*Grumbles.*) What's so good about it?

LUCIDA   You must be the new girl. Hi, I'm Lucida.

(*She smiles and extends her hand to shake.*)

OBSCURA   I'm Obscura. (*Loftily.*) I don't shake hands. (*Beat; elaborates.*) I might break.

(LUCIDA *retracts her hand.*)

LUCIDA   Okay . . . no offense.

OBSCURA   (*Haughtily.*) None taken.

(*Beat.*)

LUCIDA   (*Conspiratorially.*) You might want to avoid Norman, on the end.

  (*She points to the end of the shelf.*)

  He has a "reputation."

OBSCURA   Reputation for what?

LUCIDA   Let's just say that any vase that gets too close to him, mysteriously winds up on the floor. Norman claims it's because of earthquakes, (*Ominously.*) but we haven't had any earthquakes lately. (*Beat.*) So, how was your trip over here?

OBSCURA   (*Angrily.*) That stupid FedEx guy almost dropped me. Can you imagine? The idiot!

LUCIDA   I'm sure the glassblower wrapped you very carefully in bubble wrap. That's how he wraps all of us vases.

OBSCURA   (*Haughtily.*) Well, he should have taken more precautions with *me*. (*Preening.*) *I'm* very valuable, you know.

LUCIDA   (*Kindly.*) All the glassblower's creations are special and valuable.

OBSCURA   Well, especially me, after all that I've been through!

LUCIDA   What's that?

OBSCURA   (*Dramatically.*) Oh, the pain, the pain! After going through the fire, I thought that my trial was finally over. But, no! After I cooled down, he picked me up and started scraping away my skin! Can you *imagine*? There was no purpose for it at all. Totally uncalled for! And the worst part is, he was *smiling* the whole time, like he enjoyed it! I don't know why he has such a good reputation. There must be better glassblowers than him.

LUCIDA   He's the best, trust me. All his creations sell out almost immediately.

OBSCURA   So, how long have *you* been here?

LUCIDA   This is my third day. A buyer came yesterday but he didn't have enough money to purchase me. I heard him say something about increasing his credit limit to afford me. He's supposed to come back today.

OBSCURA   *Afford* you? How much do you cost?

LUCIDA   (*Thoughtfully.*) That's a good question. I have no idea.

OBSCURA   You must have a price tag somewhere. Let's see.

(SHE *stands and gestures for* LUCIDA *to stand.* LUCIDA *stands and* OBSCURA *begins examining* LUCIDA's *head.*)

A little dust on top here!

(*She blows on* LUCIDA*s hair.*)

LUCIDA   (*Anxiously.*) It can't be! I'm still new!

OBSCURA   I'm just pulling your leg—(*Beat; explaining.*)— figuratively speaking, of course.

LUCIDA   Of course.

OBSCURA   Let me see your bottom—

LUCIDA   EXCUSE ME?

OBSCURA   —I mean the bottom of your feet. Maybe the price tag's there.

(LUCIDA *picks up one foot, then the other, displaying the soles of her shoes.*)

No, not there, either.

(*She suddenly notices the light emanating from* LUCIDA's *body.*)

Say, what's that?

Lucida   What's what?

Obscura   That—light . . . why, you're *glowing!*

Lucida   Glowing?

(*She looks down at her body.*)

Am I? You can see me better than I can see myself . . . So, I'm not totally opaque anymore?

Obscura   No! (*Gesturing.*) You have a stripe down your side, and light is spilling out. You're glowing from the *inside!*

Lucida   (*To herself.*) So *that's* what happened.

Obscura   (*Blurts out.*) You're *so beautiful!* (*Jealously.*) How did you get that way?

Lucida   It must have been the scraping.

Obscura   You were scraped too?

Lucida   Oh, yes. I went through the fire and the scraping, just like you did.

Obscura   But you're so happy.

Lucida   Oh, I am . . . now.

Obscura   (*Excitedly.*) Lucida, do I have a light inside of *me?*

(**She** *twirls around for* **Lucida** *to examine her.* **Lucida** *looks closely.*)

Lucida   No, Obscura, you don't. I'm sorry.

Obscura   (*Pouting.*) So how come you have a light and I don't?

Lucida   I don't know.

Obscura   (*Angrily.*) That's SO unfair! If I ever see that glassblower again, I'm going to give him a piece of my mind!

Lucida   (*Thoughtfully.*) You know, Obscura, I was just like you. I didn't like going through the pain—nobody does. But when I decided to trust that the glassblower knew what he was doing, I stopped tensing up and relaxed.

OBSCURA (*Envious.*) I wish that I was glowing like you.

LUCIDA (*Comfortingly.*) I bet it's not too late. After all, the same glassblower made both of us.

(*Beat.*)

MAN'S VOICE, O.S. Hello, I've come for my vase.

WOMAN'S VOICE, O.S. Yes, sir, right here. A beautiful choice. See how it glows?

MAN'S VOICE, O.S. (*Deeply touched.*) It's exquisite! My wife is recovering from surgery and this vase will warm her spirit. Thank you!

(LUCIDA *moves as if being lifted off the shelf; She calls to* OBSCURA.)

LUCIDA Bye, bye, Obscura! I wish you the best!

(OBSCURA, *struck by the knowledge of* LUCIDA*'s purpose, waves as* LUCIDA *exits.*)

OBSCURA Bye, Lucida! (*Pause; she laments to herself.*) I'm never going to be chosen. I don't glow. I'm just an ordinary vase. I'm not "exquisite" at all. I'm just going to sit here my whole life, gathering dust—

(*A crash is heard, the sound of breaking glass; she shudders.*)

—unless Norman gets to me first. (*Beat; change of heart; yearning.*) If only I glowed, I could be a special gift for somebody, like Lucida is. (*Beat.*) I wish I could tell the glassblower that, (*Sniffles.*) but I'll never see him again.

(*She begins to sob quietly.*)

It's just too late.

(*Lights gradually fade to black.* SHE *continues to sob quietly for a long time, then footsteps are heard in the darkness.*)

Who is it? Who's there? (*Beat; softly.*) Oh, it's *you!*

(*Suddenly, a flickering light turns on inside of her and* SHE *glows.*)

END OF PLAY

CLOCK

Scott McCrea

CHARACTERS

PETER: Mid- to late 20s.
JOY: Mid- to late 20s.

TIME

The present.

SETTING

An apartment.

———————

(*A table and two chairs.* PETER *is at the table, opening a UPS package with a box cutter.* JOY *looks on.*)

PETER   It's one of those goddamn clocks. I can't believe her. What was your mother thinking? She knows we hate hers.

JOY   (*Lifting it out of the box.*) I think it's beautiful.

PETER   Beautiful? What are you saying? Are you saying you want keep it? You don't want to get rid of it?

JOY   Why should we?

PETER   The one at your mother's kept us up all night, remember? You said you hated it.

JOY   I know, but this is a gift. I want it.

PETER   You want to start it?

JOY   Yes.

PETER   But it makes all that noise.

JOY   So?

PETER   So? I work at home. I need quiet. I can't have this annoying metronome clop-clop-clopping all day long. It'll drive me crazy.

JOY   It's from my mother. I want it.

PETER   You don't have to listen to it all day.

Joy   Maybe I will . . . Maybe I'll be the one who's home.

Peter   What are you talking about?

(*Pause.*)

Joy   I'm pregnant.

Peter   You are?

Joy   Yes.

Peter   You're sure?

Joy   Yes.

Peter   Oh . . . You took the test?

Joy   Twice.

Peter   Good. 'Cause, you know, you can get a false positive.

Joy   I double-checked.

Peter   Well . . . this changes things. Changes our life. We'll have to—adjust. We'll need money. We'll have to feed it. Give it constant attention. I'll have to get a real job. With a company. Give up on my dream of my own business. But I guess that's what happens sometimes. Sometimes God wants you to forget about yourself. And what you want. And He puts you in a CAGE FOR THE REST OF YOUR LIFE!

(*Pause.*)

Joy   I could get an abortion.

Peter   Yes. Yes, you could.

Joy   Do you want me to?

Peter   I want you to do what you want . . . it's your body; it's got to be your decision. I can't make that decision for you. You're the one who has to go through with it. Whatever you decide . . . . But I can't promise I'll be here. After it's born. I can't promise I won't run away. I know myself. I don't know if I'll be able to stand it.

(*Pause.*)

JOY   I'll call to set up an appointment.

PETER   For an abortion?

JOY   Yes.

PETER   You would do that? I mean—are you sure?

JOY   I'm not raising a kid by myself. And you don't want it.

PETER   You know, when you said the word abortion, when you first said the word, I felt this wave of relief come over me. Isn't that sad? . . . I don't even have the guts to be a father.

JOY   I want you to do something.

PETER   Anything.

JOY   I want you to start the clock.

PETER   Anything you want.

(*He quickly starts to wind it.*)

JOY   I want to keep it.

(*A loud tick tock is heard.*)

(*The lights fade. In the darkness the loud tick tock continues.*)

(*The lights come up.* PETER *is at the table, typing on a laptop. The clock is on an end table several feet away. He looks up at it, seething. He crosses to it and reaches out to stop it. But he doesn't dare.*)

PETER   Goddamnit!

(JOY *enters.*)

PETER   I can't stand it. I can't stand it, Joy. I have to stop the clock.

JOY   It's the only thing I asked for.

PETER   I know. And I can't even give you that. I can't take it. It's like it's the heartbeat of our dead son. It's like "The Tell-Tale Heart." I dreamed last night I was chased all over the apartment by a fetus. Please. Please let me stop it.

(*Pause.*)

JOY   Okay.

(*He runs to the clock and stops it. The loud tick tock stops.*)

PETER   I can't even give you this. I can't even let you have one thing . . . How can you stand me?

(*Pause.*)

PETER   Say something.

(*Pause.*)

PETER   Say something.

(*Pause.*)

JOY   I stand you because when I look at you, my heart speeds up. I stand you because you're the only person that ever made me smile. Because when I go to work in the morning, I know I'm helping someone I regard as the other half of me. Why I stay is not a mystery. The real question is why do you. You don't love me so why do you stay? That's the question you don't ask yourself. You don't ask because you're afraid of the answer.

PETER   I do love you.

JOY   You stay for what you can take from me. And if I lose my job, if I give you less sex, you'll go. That's what I live with. That knowledge.

PETER   I'm not leaving you.

JOY   You will. When I can't say yes anymore, you will.

PETER   Is that what you think of me?

(JOY *looks at the clock and wipes a tear from her cheek. She picks up the clock and exits.*)

(*The lights fade.*)

END OF PLAY

CUSTOMER SUPPORT

Tom Baum

CHARACTERS

NATHAN: A white American man, age 30–50.
NASRUL: An East Indian man, age 30–50.

SETTING

The two men are seen sitting at their computers, separated by 8,000 miles.

TIME

The present.

(*Lights up on* NATHAN *at his computer,* NASRUL *at his.*)

NATHAN   What do you need, my express service code or my concierge number?

NASRUL   Please, the express service code. That will be most helpful.

NATHAN   277 . . . 191 . . . 026 . . . 98.

NASRUL   And what may I assist you with?

NATHAN   OK. This is the fourth time I'm calling about this problem. Do you have a record of my previous calls?

NASRUL   I will endeavor to find it now.

NATHAN   No, don't endeavor, I need this solved. Here's the thing. Various features of Chrome will drop out for no apparent reason, in the middle of a session. I reboot and the problem goes away and then it comes back, randomly, no warning.

NASRUL   I am sorry to hear you are having this issue and I will be solving it today. If we are disconnected, may I call you back at this number?

NATHAN   Yeah yeah. Can we skip the pleasantries in your script? I'm really slammed.

NASRUL   I will do my best to comply with your wishes. May I know to whom I have the pleasure of speaking today?

NATHAN   I'm Nathan. Today and every day.

NASRUL   I am Nasrul.

NATHAN   Well, Nasrul, I'm counting on you to fix the problem. God knows Bhabani, Deepak, and Gourab couldn't.

NASRUL   I am sorry to hear you are having such difficulties.

NATHAN   Don't apologize. Just make my system work.

NASRUL   (*Tightly.*) That is my goal and my sincerest hope. May I have the honor of sharing your screen?

NATHAN   I'm way ahead of you. Entering "custsup1" in the address box. Click yes. Open. Now I need the code.

NASRUL   The code is 105—

NATHAN   105—

NASRUL   —5772.

NATHAN   5772. Press OK. "Nasrul is sharing your screen." I'm putting you on speaker, Nasrul.

NASRUL   If you need to X out of anything, please do so now.

NATHAN   Did it already. Can we please get this done?! I'm ready to buy a new computer and it won't be this brand.

NASRUL   (*Tightly.*) That is of course your prerogative. I will first eliminate your temporary files. Yes. All right. I see. Oh.

NATHAN   Oh?

NASRUL   These are perhaps the source of the problem.

NATHAN   Which?

NASRUL   I would venture to say you have a virus as a result of visiting these sites, and I will now download Superscan to isolate it.

NATHAN Which sites?

NASRUL There. Where the cursor is.

NATHAN You're very quick with the cursor. Right, I thought I cleared history.

NASRUL There is no "clearing history." Clearing history is a canard. You are lucky to escape with just a virus.

NATHAN What could be worse than a virus?

NASRUL I will tell you what could be worse. In my country it is illegal to see such sites.

NATHAN Really? That sucks. I mean it's surprising.

NASRUL Why does this surprise you?

NATHAN Well . . . the Kama Sutra and all that.

NASRUL Yes. At one time we led the world in sexual wisdom, but no more.

NATHAN Anyway, these are old sites. Haven't been on them for a long time.

NASRUL I see they are date-stamped this morning, but I will take your word for it. What is this one?

NATHAN Which one?

NASRUL Where the cursor is.

NATHAN No idea. Why do you want to know? Please get rid of them and move on.

NASRUL I will eliminate all the evidence, and even my government could not convict you.

NATHAN Whoa. Are we talking about jail time?

NASRUL A very stiff sentence.

NATHAN So to speak.

NASRUL   Yes, ha ha, I understand. You should thank God you're an American. In my country, wives have been known to inform on their husbands for such activity.

NATHAN   Oh yeah? Not my wife. If you can't beat 'em, join 'em.

NASRUL   This is not in the Kama Sutra.

NATHAN   For all the good it did us. It was the only thing we had in common. I tried to interest her in basketball, but she kept falling asleep.

NASRUL   At least you had sexual activity. My Aishani was more interested in basketball.

NATHAN   She held out on you, huh?

NASRUL   For weeks at a time. And then sued me for divorce, citing my interest in pornography as a sign of mental illness.

NATHAN   Megan made me go to rehab. It was either that or divorce.

NASRUL   And did that save your marriage?

NATHAN   Well . . . apparently nothing can scare me off porn.

NASRUL   Ah, I see.

NATHAN   Short of tying me down and making me watch masturbating women being beheaded.

NASRUL   Please don't give my government ideas. (*Pause.*) Masturbating women, I take it that's your preference?

NATHAN   I'm fairly eclectic, but yeah, I'll cop to that.

NASRUL   I like hairy women myself.

NATHAN   I have no problem with that either.

NASRUL   Of which there is an abundance in my country.

NATHAN   We're running a shortage.

NASRUL   Aishani was so angry when she caught me. "Why do you risk imprisonment looking at such women, when you are free to look at me?"

NATHAN   They just don't get it, do they.

NASRUL   I said, "Aishani, I haven't seen you naked in a month."

NATHAN   I pleaded with Megan not to wax. She called me a dork.

NASRUL   My heart goes out to you, Nathan. But Superscan has resolved your issue.

NATHAN   Well, thank you, Nasrul.

NASRUL   Have I met with your expectations?

NATHAN   And then some. Sorry I went off on you before.

NASRUL   I have heard far worse, believe me.

NATHAN   Wish I could do something for you. Besides give you a good review.

NASRUL   There is something else you can do for me.

NATHAN   Name it.

NASRUL   While I am sharing your screen, would you mind going on a certain site? I cannot myself, without calling down the authorities. But if it is you who moves the cursor, I am beyond the reach of our laws.

NATHAN   Even though this conversation is being recorded?

NASRUL   Oh that is another canard.

NATHAN   Wow, that's good to know.

NASRUL   *Praakrtik aurat.*

NATHAN   Excuse me?

NASRUL   That is the name of the site. In English, "Natural Woman." P,R, double A,K,R,T,I,K A,U,R,A,T

NATHAN   Got it. *Praakrtik—*

NASRUL   —*aurat.*

NATHAN   Oh. I see what you mean.

NASRUL   Takes me back.

NATHAN   (*Marveling.*) Me too.

NASRUL   Nothing Brazilian about her.

NATHAN   Brazilian's for pedophiles.

NASRUL   This does not make you uncomfortable? Two men sharing a woman, as it were?

NATHAN   Hey, rock stars do it.

NASRUL   Ah, look what she's doing there.

NATHAN   Fantastic move.

NASRUL   I am indebted to you, Nathan.

NATHAN   Same here, Nasrul. Sorry I went off on you before.

NASRUL   Not to worry. I hear such outbursts every single day.

NATHAN   Americans suck ass.

NASRUL   But America is great.

NATHAN   If our wives could see us now, right, Nasrul?

NASRUL   Nathan, my friend . . . they would divorce us all over again.

(*Both men are staring at their screens, breathing more and more heavily, as the lights fade.*)

END OF PLAY

DATED HUMOR

Ken Preuss

Dated Humor was first performed in April 2016 at Orlando, Florida's Lowndes Shakespeare Center as part of Valencia College's Errors of Comedy student-directed one act showcase. The production was directed by Tim Beltley with Rob Davis as Ross and Amber Valois as Rachel.

CHARACTERS

Ross: (Male) A college student eagerly and awkwardly using comedy to impress his blind date.

Rachel: (Female) A college student with confusing and surprising reactions to her date's humor.

TIME

Present day.

SETTING

A table in a restaurant called Hungry Hewie's Hotdog Hut.

————————

(*At rise:* Ross *sits at a casual restaurant table. There is a paper cup housing plastic utensils.*)

Ross   (*Into his phone.*) I know I've had bad blind dates in the past, but I've got this. I read a BuzzFeed article about being funny on a first date. I make her laugh and we could fall in love. (*A beat, then defensively.*) I can be *funny.* Well, I'm going to follow the BuzzFeed suggestions. I've got pop-culture riffs planned. I've got a hilarious joke I found on Reddit. I've even got an awesome anecdote from high school. If all else fails, I'll do some impressions. (*Defensively.*) I don't know. I'll make cute animal noises or something. (*Answers a question.*) We're meeting at Hungry Hewie's Hotdog Hut. No. That's not part of the plan to be funny. (Rachel *enters.*) I see her! Gotta go. (*Stands and extends his hand.*) Hi. I'm Ross.

Rachel   (*Shakes his hand.*) It's nice to meet you in person. Rachel.

Ross   (*Gestures for her to sit. She does. He sits, too.*) Ross and Rachel. We're like *Friends.*

Rachel   Well, we could be. We've only just met.

Ross   I mean, we're like *Friends*, the TV show. Ross and Rachel? (*Getting flustered.*) Not that I'm saying that we *should be* friends. I mean, we *can be.* Friendship's important in any relationship. Not that we *have* a relationship. And I'm not assuming we will. I'm just saying that in case this date could *lead* to a relationship, I don't want you thinking I tried to friend-zone you one minute after we met.

RACHEL   I'd never think that.

ROSS   Great.

RACHEL   It's only been thirty seconds.

ROSS   (*A beat.*) Can we start over then? Let's use our middle names. It'll eliminate any predetermined pop culture–related relationship awkwardness. (*Stands and extends his hand as before.*) Hi. I'm Luke.

RACHEL   (*Stands and shakes his hand.*) Leia. (*She sits and opens her menu.*)

(ROSS *considers saying something, decides against it and sits. There is an awkward beat as he waits for her to look up. He gets an idea and breaks the silence by laughing to himself—rather unconvincingly—yet loudly enough for her to hear. He waits for her to glance his way then he feigns nonchalance.*)

ROSS   Oh. Sorry. I was just thinking about a joke I heard the other day. It was quite amusing. (*Before she responds.*) A Mormon, a Muslim, a Buddhist, and an atheist walk into a bar.

RACHEL   Together?

ROSS   What?

RACHEL   They walk in together?

ROSS   Yes.

RACHEL   So, they were hanging out beforehand?

ROSS   What do you mean?

RACHEL   I mean, if they're walking into a bar at the same time, they were obviously together as a group elsewhere and decided to move the party to a new location. (*More to herself.*) I guess, it's possible they planned to meet up at the bar at an appointment time. (*To him.*) Maybe it's a weekly thing. You know, for religious discussion and debate. (*To* HERSELF *again.*) But then, why choose a bar?

ROSS   (*A little impatient, but not angrily.*) I don't think they know each other.

RACHEL   So, they just randomly converged on the same place at the same time from four different locations? That's a humorous happenstance ripe with comedic potential. Please continue.

ROSS   (*A beat then he continues.*) Okay. So, a Mormon, a Muslim, a Buddhist, and an atheist walk into a bar. (*He opens his mouth to continue, but pauses.*) Wait. This isn't going to inadvertently offend you, is it?

RACHEL   Of course not. You're telling the joke *on purpose*.

ROSS   Right. (*A beat.*) Wait. What? (*A beat.*) You know, we should just order. Religion's a sensitive topic. (*Playfully pious.*) One should not find joy in belittling another's belief. Unless it's . . . Scientology. Amirite? (*Laughs as he peruses the menu.*) It amazes me what some people choose to worship.

RACHEL   Like cabbage?

ROSS   (*Glances up.*) I love it! (*Points to menu.*) I usually get the coleslaw *and* the sauerkraut.

RACHEL   No. You said, you were amazed by what some people worship, so I said, "Like cabbage."

ROSS   Yes! I've heard about that! (*With mock spookiness.*) "The Cult of the Cabbage Heads." (*Laughing.*) Can you imagine the nutcases chanting at the altar while the sacred vegetable rots and wilts?

RACHEL   That would be ridiculous.

ROSS   (*Laughing.*) I know!

RACHEL   (*With deep reverence.*) We believe each cabbage to be equally sacred.

ROSS   (*Laughter stops.*) Excuse me?

RACHEL   Each cabbage is a complex, multilayered sphere radiating goodness to soothe the soul and free the spirit.

ROSS   (*Trying to figure her out.*) So, you . . .

RACHEL   (*Pointedly, as she closes the menu.*) . . . will not be trying the coleslaw and the sauerkraut.

ROSS   (*A frantic smile as he tries to redirect her.*) There are lots of *other* items on the menu!

RACHEL   Are these items *also* created from the shredded carcasses of my sacred deities?

ROSS   Just the fused carcasses of slaughtered cows! No worries. Unless you're Hindu. (*A nervous laugh.*) Honestly, the hot dogs are great. I promise. I've got a funny story about them, too. (*Begins quickly.*) A couple of buddies and I went to Luther High School.

RACHEL   (*As if she's misunderstood the name.*) *Loser* High School?

ROSS   (*Politely correcting her.*) *Luther.* It's just around the corner. Anyway. The summer before our senior year, we decided to prank our rivals. There's this swanky private school called Werner Academy, but we used to call it *Wiener* Academy.

RACHEL   *Winner* and *Loser.* Convenient names for rivals.

ROSS   (*A little frustrated.*) Not *winner. Weiner.* I mean, *Werner,* really, but we called them Wiener. Like a *hot dog.* (*Getting back to the story.*) The point is that early in the summer, my friends and I all got jobs here at Hungry Hewey's. Every day, all summer, each chance we got, we slipped an extra wiener down our pants or into our pockets and snuck it home. A couple dogs a day—so Hewey never noticed—and by end of the summer, we'd stashed 472 wieners in a cooler in my tool shed. (*Slowly and dramatically.*) Right next to a massive homemade slingshot able to launch 60 dogs at a time.

(*Quickly again.*) Fast forward a few months . . . (*Stands and gestures grandly.*) Weiner Academy Grad Night 2014 (*Really into it, pointing and acting things out.*) Their entire senior class is on the football field, the band is playing the alma mater, and—from the roof of the Piggly Wiggly—we attack. Eight quick shots. Impeccably choreographed, perfectly executed . . . (*With a grand flourish.*) and wieners were raining from the heavens. (*A genuine laugh.* HE *really finds it funny.*) They didn't know what hit them! I mean, they did know. It was *wieners.* But they had no clue where they came from. It was hilarious.

RACHEL   The legendry wiener storm was *you* and *your friends*? I remember that!

ROSS   Awesome? Where did you go to high school?

RACHEL   (*Dryly.*) Werner Academy. Class of 2014. I was in the band.

ROSS   I thought you lived at the beach.

RACHEL   Well, I moved to the beach after I dropped out.

ROSS   Of college?

RACHEL   High school. By Grad Night, I'd already planned to go to Julliard, but the following week, my musical audition was a complete disaster. I couldn't play a correct note, lost my scholarship, became depressed, gave up on school, and ran away. When I ran out of cash, I dismantled my sousaphone to sell as scrap metal and found a hotdog wedged inside.

ROSS   I am . . . so sorry.

RACHEL   No worries. Wasn't like I became homeless. I lived beneath a lifeguard stand on the beach and got part-time work on the boardwalk as a vomit-removal technician.

ROSS   (*There is a beat of stunned silenced. Desperate to make her laugh, he grabs two plastic knives, holding them to his lips like tusks.*) Look. I'm a walrus! (*Grunts comically.*)

Rachel   (*Deadpanned.*) My father was killed by a walrus.

Ross   (*His grunts turn to gasps.*) What?

Rachel   It happened last week. He sought me out to mend our broken relationship. We were about to embrace in the boardwalk aquarium when the massive mammal escaped an exhibit and impaled him with his razor-sharp tusks.

Ross   (*To himself.*) This cannot get any worse.

Rachel   It can. The carnage was so gruesome that the tourists began getting sick. As a vomit-removal technician, I was forced to clean their regurgitated lunches from the crime scene. Ironically, it consisted chiefly of hotdogs. (*Beat. Then a smile.*) Shall we order?

Ross   (*Stands quickly.*) No! I have to go. Everything I've said has been horribly wrong. Forgive me. (*Exits.*)

Rachel   (*Watches him go. Dials cell phone.*) Hi, Gracie. It's me. (*Beat.*) It's over. He ran out. I don't get it. I made jokes about everything he said. (*Beat.*) Stupid BuzzFeed article!

End of Play

DEVELOPING

Marj O'Neill-Butler

CHARACTERS

LAURA: 30s, Mindy's mom, wise, quick, humorous, tall.
GWEN: 30s, Poppy's mom, busty, good friend to Laura.
CONNIE: Mid-30s, Rosie's mom, nosy, negative, rumor monger.

TIME

After school.

SETTING

A bench outside a middle school.

———————

(*Two friends,* LAURA *and* GWEN, *are waiting on a bench outside a middle school.*)

LAURA   Mindy got her period last night.

GWEN   Wow. That's early.

LAURA   Barely twelve. I mean, we've talked about it, but I didn't think she was ready yet.

GWEN   Was she scared?

LAURA   Not in the least. She actually bragged. About how she'd be the first in her group. I remember hiding the fact when I got it.

GWEN   Me too. Sneaking into the girls' room at school. Making excuses why I was taking so long. And the pads. Afraid they'd leak.

LAURA   And they always did. In my high school this popular girl Claire won an award at assembly. She walked up to get it and the whole room was gasping because she had this huge red spot on the back of her skirt. I mean huge.

GWEN   How awful. She must have been so embarrassed.

LAURA   Probably not. She was one of the really cool smart kids. Nothing seemed to faze her.

GWEN I was never like that. Everything that wasn't normal made me crazy. I would've left that school if it were me.

LAURA Mindy doesn't get bothered by things like that.

GWEN You've raised her right then. I hope Poppy is like her.

LAURA She will be.

GWEN She adores Mindy. It's "Mindy got all A's." "Mindy won her soccer game."

LAURA That's sweet. She'll be fine.

GWEN I hope so. She's so shy.

LAURA She'll come out of it. Get her involved in sports or something.

GWEN She doesn't like sports. Says she hates the competition.

LAURA She'll find something she likes.

GWEN Rob has no patience with her. Says she needs to put herself out there.

LAURA Some kids can't at this age. I think being tall held me back somewhat. But I was observant. Watched how things were done. I still remember at this middle school dance how this girl Carol floated from one guy to the next as each dance ended. And she was so pretty and smart all the boys danced with her without question. And she didn't care if they were the popular guys. She just wanted to dance.

GWEN Imagine being that self-possessed. I'm still not to this day. Except maybe with Rob. He's always made me feel . . . wanted. Special.

LAURA That's good. To be deemed special.

(CONNIE *rushes in.*)

CONNIE Laura, I need to talk. It's urgent.

LAURA What's up?

CONNIE   Sorry, it's a bit private.

(GWEN *starts to leave.*)

LAURA   That's okay. Don't go, Gwen.

CONNIE   Okay but . . . this is kind of personal. It's about Mindy.

LAURA   (*Alert.*) What's happened?

CONNIE   She's not in danger. Yet. But . . . oh God, I don't know how to tell you this.

LAURA   Clearly you want to, so go ahead.

CONNIE   Okay. Rosie was in the girls' room today and saw Mindy. She was . . . lifting her shirt up and showing her chest.

LAURA   And?

CONNIE   She was showing her boobs.

GWEN   Mindy has boobs?

LAURA   Not really. Sort of little rosebuds.

GWEN   She must be so excited.

LAURA   Probably why she was showing them off.

CONNIE   Rosie said the girls were all laughing.

LAURA   And why not? They're all going to develop soon. Mindy's just ahead of the game.

CONNIE   She's not. My Rosie has huge boobs. She tapes them down every morning.

GWEN   And you let her.

CONNIE   Of course. I don't want her to be embarrassed.

LAURA   Clearly she is, if she came running to you about Mindy.

CONNIE   But . . . I don't want her showing her body to everyone.

LAURA   How many girls were there? In the girls' room?

CONNIE   I don't know.

LAURA   They were probably her friends. Sharing a moment.

CONNIE   Why would you think that's okay?

GWEN   Oh right! Hide them under some tape. Pretend she's still a baby.

CONNIE   That's not what Rosie's doing.

LAURA   Yes, it is. What she needs is a proper fitting bra.

CONNIE   That would be worse. She doesn't want them sticking out.

GWEN   They're called breasts, Connie. Or boobs. Not "them."

LAURA   She needs a bra that minimizes her shape if she's big. It'll be better for her in the end. If she keeps taping her breasts down, they'll lose their lift. And when she's eighteen and into boys, she'll hate that.

GWEN   And why doesn't she want them sticking out? I thought all girls yearned for breasts.

LAURA   It's not a matter of wanting them anyway. It's the natural way. Their bodies develop as they age. Why should they be ashamed about their bodies?

GWEN   (*To* CONNIE.) Has Rosie ever seen you naked?

CONNIE   Of course not. A little modesty goes a long way.

GWEN   Maybe that's why she hiding her breasts. She thinks that's normal.

CONNIE   It's not normal to lift your shirt in the girls' room.

LAURA   Should I shame her? Is that what you think I should do? I'm sorry this has upset you, Connie. But it's none of your business. Or Rosie's. I have taught Mindy to be open about her body. That a person's body is not shameful. That each phase of her life is to be celebrated. I'm sure I'm not going to change your mind. But if any rumors start about Mindy and her breasts, I'll know where they came from.

CONNIE   I was only trying to help.

(CONNIE *starts to leave.*)

LAURA   No, you were hoping to start trouble.

(CONNIE *leaves.*)

GWEN   I'll bet she's never talked to Rosie about the birds and the bees.

LAURA   Of course not. That's too dirty. Let the kid find out on her own, like she did.

GWEN   Rosie is going to be so screwed up. I bet the taping was Connie's idea.

LAURA   Where do people get these ideas? And why is it always with females? You never hear of guys taping down their dicks so they don't show.

GWEN   Maybe they do and we don't know about it. Sex! Why can't people just leave it alone and enjoy it?

LAURA   Poor Rosie. She's either going to be frigid or become the town bicycle.

GWEN   Laura!

LAURA   Tell me I'm not right. It's always the prudes who turn out to be loose.

GWEN   Either way, I think Connie is going to have her hands full.

LAURA   Connie probably hides in her closet when getting undressed.

GWEN   You're awful!

LAURA   I'm not. I'm a realist. She's a prude. Let me tell you about this book I bought for Mindy. You're going to need it before you know. We don't want Poppy to be like Rosie. And looking at your boobs, she's going to be an early developer.

GWEN   Why are you looking at my boobs?

LAURA   Because they're there. Happily underneath your sweater.

GWEN   Maybe Poppy will be like Mindy, with little rosebuds.

LAURA   Not a chance, Mama. Just like you, she's going to have the whole big bush. So to speak.

GWEN   You're so naughty. And fun. That's why I like you.
(*She looks off right.*)
Here they come. Look at Poppy. She adores Mindy.

LAURA   Let's take them for ice cream and celebrate. Make it a party, so Poppy can find out.

GWEN   She'll think she's died and gone to heaven. Learning about Mindy. Thanks Laura.

(*They exit while waving to the girls off stage.*)

LAURA   Who wants ice cream?

END OF PLAY

THE FALLING OF THE CRANES

John McKinney

The Falling of the Cranes was first presented as part of an overnight writing challenge at Manhattan Theatre Source on MacDougall Street in New York City in 2007. It was further developed at the Workshop Theater in 2010 as part of a collection of short plays entitled *Attention Deficit Drama*, after which it has been given several public readings by other New York theater companies.

Workshop Theater cast:

MARYANNE: Ellen Barry

ELLIE: Sutton Crawford

Director: John McKinney

CHARACTERS

MARIANNE: Ellie's mom. 40's, maternal, caring, doting. The perfect mother, but with a dark secret.

ELLIE: Marianne's daughter. 15, wide-eyed, eager, good natured, but with memories of a not-always happy childhood.

TIME

Summer, morning.

SETTING

A cottage by a lake.

(*A cottage. Summer.* ELLIE *is asleep in a chair. She wakes up and begins to take in her surroundings.*)

ELLIE   No way!

(*She gets up and begins to explore the room. She appears to recognize the place.* MARIANNE *enters carrying a mug and sets it down on a table.*)

Oh my god, I don't believe it!

MARIANNE   (*Cheerful.*) Good morning. Glad to see you're finally awake. You slept well, I trust?

ELLIE   (*As if surprised to see her.*) Mom. (*Bewildered, pacing.*) Yes. Very well, but—

MARIANNE   It's so nice to see you up on your feet. I knew those doctors were a bunch of quacks. They said you'd never get out of bed again, but look at you! You're like a five-year-old again! What is it?

ELLIE   I . . . I can't believe we're here!

MARIANNE   You recognize the place then?

ELLIE   Yes! Of course! It's the cottage by the lake, where you used to bring me when I was a kid.

MARIANNE   You do remember.

ELLIE   Yeah, but . . . how did I get here? It's weird, I don't remember anything.

MARIANNE   Well, I'm not surprised. You were sound asleep when we arrived. Just like when you were little. You always used to fall asleep in the car, remember?

ELLIE   Right! And then I'd wake up here the next morning . . . wondering how I got here . . . and there you'd be . . . bringing me cocoa. So how long did you rent the cottage for? The summer?

MARIANNE   Or longer, if you like. It's all ours, now.

ELLIE   You mean you *bought it*? When?! Why didn't you tell me?

MARIANNE   I wanted it to be a surprise.

ELLIE   Oh my god! Really! (*Excited, looking around.*) I always dreamed of coming back here one day but—(*Looking out the window.*) Ohh, the lake! It's just as beautiful as ever. Oh my gosh, I don't believe it! There's that old tire swing! After all these years! It's still there!

MARIANNE   It's nice to see you so happy again. You were always happy here, weren't you? Well. Except for hunting season.

ELLIE   Hunting season?

MARIANNE   Every so often you'd be watching the cranes flying over the lake . . . and there'd be a gunshot . . . and one of the cranes would fall out of the sky, into the water. You used to cry and cry . . . used to break my heart.

ELLIE   And you used to cheer me up by sitting me on your lap and singing me a lullaby.

MARIANNE   You remember.

(*Pause.*)

ELLIE   What did you mean, about the doctors?

MARIANNE   Excuse me?

ELLIE   You mentioned doctors before. How they said I'd never get out of bed again . . . .

MARIANNE   Oh, that. You really don't remember being in the hospital?

ELLIE   Oh right. It's coming back to me. I was there for a while, right? Like, days . . . .

MARIANNE   Uh-huh. They were running some tests on you. To find out why you were so tired all the time.

ELLIE   Right, and I remember you and everyone getting all worried for some reason.

(*Remembering.*)

I had an operation!

MARIANNE   Yes.

ELLIE   But I can't remember any more than that. Why is that?

MARIANNE   All the drugs they were giving you, no doubt. Affected your memory. But don't worry. Things'll come back to you, in time. How do you feel, otherwise?

ELLIE   Good. Great. I'm not tired at all now! So I guess everything turned out all right?

MARIANNE   Everything's turned out wonderful.

ELLIE   So what happened? What was wrong with me? How long was I in the hospital?

MARIANNE   So many questions. It's your first day back. We'll have plenty of time to talk about it later. Why don't we talk about what do you want to do tomorrow?

ELLIE   What I want to do?

MARIANNE   Would you like to go for a swim? Or maybe a bike ride? Or go butterfly hunting. We used to love doing that, remember?

ELLIE   No we didn't.

MARIANNE   What?

ELLIE   I always used to ask if we could go butterfly hunting but we never did.

MARIANNE   Okay, well, if you still want to do that, we can. Whatever you want to do, Ellie, that's what I want to do, too!

(*Pause.*)

ELLIE   Mom, what's going on?

MARIANNE   What do you mean?

ELLIE   Come on. You haven't paid this kind of attention to me since—since dad left.

MARIANNE   Honey, I'm just—

ELLIE   (*Stressing the point.*) *Because* dad left.

MARIANNE   What? No, that's not tr—

ELLIE   Oh, please. I may have been five years old but I wasn't blind. He left us, and you blamed me for it.

MARIANNE   No, don't say th—

ELLIE   And for every other man you chased but didn't catch. I was always cramping your style, wasn't I? So forgive me if I seem a little suspicious but there's just something a little odd about your wanting to pay so much attention to me all of a sudden. What happened, huh? No, really! What momentous, apocalyptic revelation happened that could make you go from being an absentee parent for ten years to suddenly being a loving, doting mother again? Waiting on me . . . buying a cottage for me!

(*She looks around.*)

And not just buying it, but making sure it looks exactly the same as it used to. The chairs . . . the tables . . . everything's exactly as it was. A little strange, isn't it?

MARIANNE Strange?

ELLIE Even the tire swing outside! It's like nothing's changed from fifteen years ago!

(*She quickly runs off stage, then returns.*)

There's no car outside.

MARIANNE Should there be?

ELLIE I thought I fell asleep in the car. But if there's no car . . . how did you bring me here?

(*Pause.*)

Oh my god.

MARIANNE It's all right. I'm here, now. I'm going to take care of you. I know I didn't before, but I'm going to make it all up to you, I promise. You were right, there was an apocalyptic moment for me. It was the moment the doctor said that word. (*A beat.*) Leukemia. It was like a gunshot. I felt the way you did as a child, when a crane fell from the sky. I couldn't bear to see my beautiful little crane die.

ELLIE (*Shock, horror.*) The operation. It wasn't successful.

MARIANNE No.

ELLIE But you're here with me. How . . . ?

MARIANNE Like I said, I couldn't bear it. There were syringes of morphine by your bedside. When the nurses weren't looking . . . .

ELLIE Mom . . . . Oh Mom . . . .

MARIANNE It's all right. This is what I wanted. And you? Isn't this what you always wanted?

ELLIE (*A bittersweet smile.*) Yes.

MARIANNE   (*Opening her arms.*) So there's nothing to be sad about, is there?

(ELLIE *sits on* MARIANNE'*s lap, her face buried in her mother's hair to hide her tears as* MARIANNE *strokes her hair and begins to sing a soft lullaby. Lights slowly fade.*)

END OF PLAY

FATIMA HALAWANI, BUCK-WILD

Asher Wyndham

Produced originally as a ten-minute play under the title *Fatima & Maama*.

Produced in Sydney, Australia, part of Short + Sweet, January 2011. Directed by Liz Arday. Fatima was played by Pamela Ghosn, Maama by Melinda Nassif.

Part of the Chaos Festival, produced by Point of Contention Theatre Company, Chicago, November 2010. Directed by Derek Van Tessel. Fatima was played by Cheyenne Pinson, Maama by Rula Gardenier.

CHARACTERS

FATIMA HALAWANI: 15. An Iraqi-American. Not biracial. She wears big geeky eyeglasses. Can be played by someone who looks young.

MAAMA: Her mother, 40s. She is in her uniform she wears at the gas station. She is disheveled and tired. She wears a hijab. Can be played by a younger actor—why not?

TIME

Present day.

SETTING

A small apartment in Ypsilanti, Michigan, near Ann Arbor.

A kitchen table. Three chairs. Cutting board on the table with eggplant.

NOTE

Choose a song that is a chart topper but also a song that is appropriate for krumping.

(*At rise:* MAAMA *stands at the table cleaning a brown stain on her hijab and gas station uniform shirt with a kitchen rag. On the table, some eggplant on a chopping board and a knife.* FATIMA, *seated, wears big geeky glasses and a hijab. Her backpack is at her feet. She is reading* Cosmo Girl.)

MAAMA   *Cosmo Girl?* The Fuel Shop sells that. It's the girl version of that floozy magazine. Why are you staring at skimpy dresses?!

FATIMA   There's a, um, Homecoming Dance.

(*Quick like a ninja,* MAAMA *takes the magazine! And puts it in her apron pocket.*)

Everyone is goin' now. Even the Goths. Even some Muslims.

(MAAMA's *face reads* "Really"?)

Yeah. It's gonna be, like, The Event. The theme is Feelin' Groovy!

MAAMA   Feeling groovy with a guy!? You have a date!?

FATIMA   No. No boy likes Fatima Halawani—and I don't care.

MAAMA   Good. Then you don't have to go.

FATIMA   I neeeed to go. I have to show off . . . my killer dance moves. (*Takes out a DVD from her backpack.*) Just five bucks at Goodwill.

MAAMA   *Buck-Wild: A Crash Course on Krumping.* You're spending your allowance on ghetto dancing videos!? Good Muslim girls don't get their groove on!

FATIMA   Watch me take it to the streets! Yo, DJ, hit it!

(*Dance music plays.* FATIMA *starts krumping.*)

FATIMA   I'm buck-wild, right?

MAAMA   Buck-wild?? No, you're Fatima.

(MAAMA *shakes* FATIMA *back to reality, music stops.*)

MAAMA   Sit down and chop baadenjaan. (*Meaning the eggplant.*) Respect your Maama. Good and dutiful. Always.

FATIMA   AHHHH! I WANNA BE NORMAL—!

(FATIMA *stabs the eggplant and just misses her* MAAMA*'s hand!*)

MAAMA   You almost murdered Maama.

FATIMA   SOOO UN-FAIR! AAUUGH! You, you're so not like *normal* moms who, like, let their daughters do *what-ever* they want, like go to Joe's Pizza and eat atomic wings. Gimme more freedom. Don't put me in another brace. The scoliosis brace was bad enough . . . .

MAAMA   Good Muslim children, like, never chide their parents. My Lord! Bestow on Fatima thy Mercy even as she cherished me in childhood. (See the Koran, Chapter 17: Verse 23.)

FATIMA   My spine's fine now. So I wanna showcase my moves, my knowledge. I don't wanna be the "Paperbag Princess from A-rab

Land" anymore! The white chicks are right when they laugh at me. These geeky glasses—I don't want to wear them!

MAAMA   You want *a lot* of things. A dress. An iPod. Pink Yeti boots?? . . . Fatima. I want to give you more, but times are . . . hard since . . . Baaba . . . died. His Chrysler pension is not enough. Ypsilanti may be cheaper than Ann Arbor, but not much. And I got billsbillsbills.

FATIMA   I'm sorry I was born with a spine like a question mark.

MAAMA   Fatima!

FATIMA   (*Grabs her backpack and DVD, starts to exit—*) I HATE YOU!!! YOU'RE SO . . . —SO NOT AMERICAN!!! WHY DON'T YOU GO BACK TO IRAQ, YOU SLURPEE RAGHEAD!!?

(MAAMA *turns her back to* FATIMA. FATIMA *cries.* MAAMA *holds back her tears.*)

FATIMA   I'm sorry.

MAAMA   I'd like you to have fun. (*Turns to face* FATIMA.) But I don't want you to cry at the dance.

FATIMA   I won't because I'll seriously impress *everyone.* Krumping makes me . . . invincible.

MAAMA   Whenever you get made fun of, I get upset. I know how you feel. Some trucker threw Root Beer Slurpee on me, and told me to go back to where I came from.

FATIMA   If Daddy was here, he'd show up and make sure no one picked on us.

MAAMA   He's not here . . . .

FATIMA   (*After a moment.*) So you get hurt sometimes. And I'll get hurt too.

MAAMA   Yes. (*After a moment.*) Hey! How about I be your chaperone at the dance?

FATIMA   I am almost sixteen, hello!

MAAMA   I'll serve almond flan and punch.

FATIMA   (*Flat, like on life support in a hospital.*) Uhhhh, I guess it'll be all right, if you came to the dance . . . .

MAAMA   *Great.* (*After a moment.*) We'll get through this. One insult at a time, okay?

FATIMA   (*Nods, then smiles.*) Yo, DJ, gimme some muzak!

(FATIMA *krumps. Music under.*)

MAAMA   Why are you dancing if there is no music?

FATIMA   I hear music—in my head!

(FATIMA *continues krumping. After a moment,* MAAMA *mimics* FATIMA. *She's clunky.* FATIMA *laughs.*)

FATIMA   Muslim girls shouldn't get their groove on!

MAAMA   We're going to have to get our groove on, if we're going to be invincible!

(*They get buck wild!! They have fun, they start laughing, but then they get serious. They get hardcore—as if they're determined to defeat every racist in the USA—with killer dance moves. Music gets louder—so loud it would shake the walls of any small apartment—so loud they think everyone in the country is listening. If possible: Strobe lights flash like in a dance club.*)

END OF PLAY

GEOMETRY

Anton Dudley

CHARACTERS

(*Ages unimportant.*)

TRIANGLE: Male, a triangle.
SQUARE: Female, a square.
CIRCLE: Whatever you want it to be, but clearly a circle.

SETTING

Somewhere shapely.

(TRIANGLE *tries to pass through* SQUARE, *but can't and is bumped backwards.*)

SQUARE   Ow!

TRIANGLE   What?

SQUARE   Your points are too sharp!

TRIANGLE   Your box is too small!

SQUARE   Why's it always my fault?!

TRIANGLE   I'm a triangle! Triangles have points! There's nothing that says boxes have to be small!

SQUARE   Fine! . . . let's try again.

TRIANGLE   Sure! Why not? I'm sure this time, it'll be different!

(*They try again and, once more, they fail.*)

SQUARE   Ow!

TRIANGLE   You think it feels good for me?

SQUARE   I didn't say that, I was just—

TRIANGLE   'Cause it doesn't!

SQUARE   I didn't assume it did!

TRIANGLE   And you yelling "ow!" every time is *really* distracting.

SQUARE   I'm not going to hide how I feel.

TRIANGLE Obviously!

SQUARE Again?

(TRIANGLE *shrugs. Another attempt, same result.*)

TRIANGLE (*Obviously!*) Ow! Ow!

SQUARE . . . Remember when this worked?

TRIANGLE No. Again?

(SQUARE *sighs. Another attempt, same result.*)

SQUARE I'm not happy.

TRIANGLE And I am?

SQUARE You know something . . . I don't think I have anything to say to you.

TRIANGLE Not even "ow?"

SQUARE (*Pointed, with an air of victory.*) Oh, trust me. I won't be saying "ow" for a very long time.

(TRIANGLE *looks concerned.*)

(CIRCLE *enters.* CIRCLE *has curves in all the right places. Both* TRIANGLE *and* SQUARE *are transfixed.*)

TRIANGLE Whoa!

SQUARE Oh! Oh my.

CIRCLE Hey. What's shaping?

TRIANGLE Um . . . you?

SQUARE Most certainly you.

CIRCLE Aren't you both sweet?

SQUARE I've never seen you before.

TRIANGLE Yeah, you're not *edgy* at all!

CIRCLE Kinda makes your head spin, don't it?

SQUARE   Where'd you come from?

CIRCLE   Nowhere in particular.

TRIANGLE   Where're you headed?

CIRCLE   Nowhere in particular.

SQUARE   So free!

CIRCLE   That's how it is when you're on a *roll*.

TRIANGLE   Would you . . . ?

(TRIANGLE *gets shy and stops his question.*)

CIRCLE   What?

TRIANGLE   Nothing.

CIRCLE   No. Roll on.

TRIANGLE   Would you . . . mind if I . . . I mean . . . may I . . . please . . . pass through you?

SQUARE   *Really*?!

CIRCLE   Sure, go right ahead.

(TRIANGLE *passes through* CIRCLE. *It's smooth and simple.*)

TRIANGLE   Wow!

CIRCLE   Totally.

TRIANGLE   That was so easy!

CIRCLE   Felt good, right?

TRIANGLE   You, too?

CIRCLE   Set me spinning!

SQUARE   Um, may I . . . ?

CIRCLE   Sure. Pass on through.

(SQUARE *passes through* CIRCLE.)

SQUARE   Oh, Mozzarella and cheddar with sugar!

CIRCLE What?

SQUARE Sweet *cheeses*!

TRIANGLE She doesn't like to swear.

CIRCLE Nice.

(SQUARE *stares enamored at* CIRCLE.)

SQUARE How do you *do* that?

CIRCLE I just roll with the flow. See you guys *around*.

(CIRCLE *giggles and rolls off. Pause.* SQUARE *and* TRIANGLE *look at each other.*)

SQUARE Can you imagine not having straight edges?

TRIANGLE I can now.

SQUARE Sweet cheeses, what have we done?

TRIANGLE The impossible . . . we enjoyed our geometry.

SQUARE But not with each other.

TRIANGLE No. I guess not.

(*Suddenly, they both look sad and ashamed.*)

SQUARE Can you ever think well of me again?

TRIANGLE Baby, from now on? I'm thinking outside the box.

(*Blackout.*)

END OF PLAY

GRAND GENTLEMAN PIRATE BOB

Deanna Alisa Ableser

CHARACTERS

MAN: Male, age: early 20s–late 40s. Longer hair. Disheveled but handsome. Dressed in a ratty pirate costume. Facial hair is raggedy. Any ethnicity.

WOMAN: Female, age: early 20s–late 40s. Dressed comfortably. Hair and makeup nicely done. Any ethnicity. Nice-looking but plain-looking.

SETTING

Two solid black cubes. One downstage center and one upstage right.

(*A* WOMAN *enters stage and stands center stage on a block.* SHE *pulls a gold key out of her pocket and starts examining it. A* MAN *dressed in a pirate costume runs onto stage as if* HE *were being chased.* HE *stops at* WOMAN.)

MAN   (*In a pirate accent.*) Don't let them know you saw me. Don't ever let them know you saw me.

(MAN *runs and hides behind a single black cube USR.*)

WOMAN   (*Yelling after* MAN.) Excuse me?

MAN   (*From behind cube.*) Shh. You never saw me. Never.

(WOMAN *starts looking at key again and holds it up to the light.*)

WOMAN   I wonder how I got . . .

(WOMAN *is interrupted by a flutter of arrows being sent across stage.*)

WOMAN   What the . . .

(WOMAN *leans down and starts picking up an arrow.* MAN *sneaks out from behind cube, crouches right by* WOMAN *and puts a finger to* HIS *lips.*)

MAN   (*Reaching out to grab key.*) I'll be taking that from you at this point, m'lady.

WOMAN   (*Pulling key back and putting it in* HER *pocket.*) You'll be taking nothing from me. I don't even know who you are.

Man   (*Bowing.*) Grand Gentleman Pirate Bob. At your service. Somewhat.

Woman   (*Laughing.*) Pirate Bob?

Man   There is no need to laugh at me, my dearest lady. Surely you see you have been shot at by multiple arrows? Surely you fear for your life?

Woman   (*Picking up arrows and looking at them more closely.*) These are toy arrows. From the local toy store. I just got back from taking my nephew there to get a gift for a birthday party. I think they are relatively harmless. In perspective.

Man   Grand Gentleman Pirate Bob must save you. It's my duty. My sworn duty of all time. My birthright.

Woman   (*Jumping down and sitting on block.*) Look. I'm not trying to be rude or anything and I'm sure your intentions are great, but I really think I'm okay. (*Pause.*) Other than toy arrows being shot at me and a random 'pirate man' running across my path.

Man   (*Overly heartbroken.*) But I'm Pirate Bob. Grand Gentleman Pirate Bob.

Woman   You don't need to overact.

Man   (*Starting to cry.*) I was sworn to . . . .

Woman   Please don't cry. Please. I can't take it when grown men cry. Especially when they are dressed up in pirate costumes.

Man   (*Crying even more.*) But I'm . . . .

Woman   (*Interrupting.*) Grand Gentleman Pirate Bob. I know. I know. I heard you the first few times. Look, like I said, I don't mean to be rude, but I'm sure both of us have more important things to do than to sit here talking to each other, so let's just pretend that things are totally normal and none of this ever happened.

Man   (*Weakly.*) You have the key, m'lady. The key.

WOMAN   (*Pulling out key from pocket and reexamining it.*) I'm sure it's just some old toy key. I found it in my attic while I was doing some cleaning. I'm sure it belongs to . . .

MAN   (*Putting hand over her mouth.*) Shhh . . . they could hear you.

 WOMAN   (*Getting off cube and starting to walk offstage.*) I think I need to go get myself a very, very very strong espresso.

(*There are some toy arrows shot again from offstage.*)

(WOMAN *is about to get one from ground again and* MAN *throws himself in her path.*)

MAN   (*Very overdramatic.*) I must protect you from danger. I must . . .

(WOMAN *picks up another arrow and stabs it hard into* MAN.)

MAN   (*Very "girly."*) Ow.

WOMAN   I'm sure you're fine.

MAN   Double ow. Grand Gentleman Pirate Bob should not be encumbered by a single or a double ow. (*Reaching up.*) If you'd just give me the key . . . .

WOMAN   We've already been through that. I really think it's best if you just . . .

(MAN *reaches into pocket and pulls out a small treasure chest.*)

MAN   (*Very overdramatic.*) I was given this by my great-great-grandfather. He was also a Grand Gentleman Pirate. Grand Gentleman Pirate Bob. I was named after him.

WOMAN   It looks markedly like the one at that very same toy store . . .

MAN   (*Even more overdramatic.*) The key. Please.

(WOMAN *looks at the key and then at* MAN *and back again. Finally, she gives in and gives him the key. Another set of toy arrows flies across the stage and* MAN *scrambles with treasure chest and key to USR block again.* WOMAN *climbs back onto block. There are a few seconds of silence.*)

WOMAN   (*Clearing her throat meekly.*) Excuse me?

(There is no sound except for the sound of the key in the treasure chest.)

WOMAN   Grand Gentleman Pirate Bob?

MAN   *(From behind block, but weakly.)* At your service.

WOMAN   You're okay, right?

MAN   I'm fine, m'lady. Just fine.

WOMAN   Did you open it?

MAN   Yes.

(WOMAN is about to step off block to come over to MAN.)

MAN   It's really best if you stay there. I'll be more than fine.

WOMAN   Grand Gentleman Pirate Bob?

MAN   Yes.

WOMAN   The key was real, wasn't it?

MAN   Authentically so. Grand Gentleman Pirate's honor. I give you my word.

WOMAN   And the arrows? The people after you?

MAN   It's a different world now. Things change.

WOMAN   *(After a short pause.)* You're leaving now, aren't you?

MAN   I've got to return the costume by 7 p.m. *(Pulling out antique pocket watch.)* It's almost 6:30.

WOMAN   *(Picking up a toy arrow.)* I don't suppose this was all a dream.

MAN   I don't suppose so. Perhaps. *(Pause.)* It's 6:30, m'lady. It's been a pleasure.

WOMAN   Have a beautiful evening, Grand Gentleman Pirate Bob.

(MAN rushes off stage and WOMAN steps down off block and slowly starts walking opposite direction.)

(Lights fade.)

END OF PLAY

GRASS AND ANDY

INSPIRED BY AESOP'S "THE ANT AND THE GRASSHOPPER"

Jonathan Josephson

CHARACTERS

ANDY: Late 20s—works hard, a music executive.
GRASS: Late 20s—hardly works, a musician.

SETTING

Andy's office at Interscope Records.

NOTE

The author is open to both roles being played by actors of any gender. If slight modifications to gendered words (such "she" to "he," etc.) need to adjust to fit the cast in the play, that's fine.

———————————

(*Lights rise on* ANDY, *slacks and a collared shirt, sitting at his desk. To one side, there are photos with* ANDY *with famous pop musicians; across from them, a shelf of awards and commendations.*)

GRASS   Knock, knock—anybody home?

(GRASS *knocks and enters at the same time. He carries a guitar case and a backpack, and wears an elaborate hand-embroidered jacket.*)

ANDY   Yeah, who's th—hi.

GRASS   Hi to you too.

ANDY   (*To the intercom.*) Hey Marjorie—hold my calls for a little bit, thanks.

(GRASS *scopes out the office.*)

GRASS   "Hold my calls." "It's okay, he's just my deadbeat cousin."

ANDY   What are you doing here?

GRASS   Andy. Cousin. Son of my mother's brother. It's been a few years, how's life?

ANDY   I'm happy to see you, but you can't just show up here.

GRASS   Would it have been better if I showed up at your house? Mrs. wouldn't like that.

Andy   You brought your guitar?

Grass   Let's say—

Andy   I can't get you a studio gig, that isn't my department. If you want to write press releases, maybe I can help you—

Grass   Let's say I didn't have anywhere else to leave it. Anywhere.

Andy   Your apartment—

Grass   Kicked out.

Andy   The band?

Grass   Moved on.

Andy   Jeanie?

Grass   Long gone.

Andy   What about your parents?

Grass   Eff that noise.

Andy   Grass—

Grass   I have a guitar, some clothes, and that's it. But hey—how are you?

Andy   What happened?

Grass   Same, stupid story. Too many mistakes.

Andy   Who's surprised.

Grass   I'm an archetype, I know.

Andy   You couldn't be more right.

Grass   So—

Andy   Which is why I'm not going to help you.

Grass   Excuse me?

Andy   No. Cousin. The answer is no.

Grass   Wait—

ANDY   You can't borrow money, you can't stay at my house, you can't leave me your demo, you can't have a job.

GRASS   Where is this hostility coming from?

ANDY   It isn't like this is some big shock, some new phenomenon. You waste time, you don't do anything, and then the world kicks your butt!

GRASS   You don't know what happened—

ANDY   I know exactly what happened! You didn't take anything seriously, you skated by on pure talent, which thank goodness you had at least some, and then you burned every bridge, you didn't plan ahead, and now you're mad at me!

GRASS   I have AIDS.

ANDY   Oh my G-d. . . . seriously?

(*A pause.* GRASS *nods.*)

GRASS   . . . no. But wouldn't you feel totally wrecked—

ANDY   Come on!

GRASS   —you would have felt so awful if you just went all high and mighty and I came to you because I have AIDS. Which I don't.

ANDY   Grass!

GRASS   I just need a little help! (*Calming.*) Just a little. You're the guy here, you're an VP at Interscope freaking Records. You know people. You have a nice house, and a couch at least—what's the harm?

ANDY   You don't take anything seriously.

GRASS   I don't! And I'm okay with that.

ANDY   What happened?

GRASS   I was late for a gig, okay, and then I was drunk for a gig— too drunk, more drunk than I should have been—and then I slept with someone I shouldn't have—

ANDY   Sweet mother—

GRASS   She's of age, it's not that, it's the other thing. She liked how I sang. She just happened to be married. To a cop.

ANDY   You really can pick 'em.

GRASS   The cop had my apartment tossed, they found my stuff. My bad stuff. They found my bills, notified the credit card people as to where I was—so those guys came and took the rest of my stuff. They took my car, my checking account. I was locked up for 45 days. But I'm done with that. I am being serious now. I'm taking this seriously.

ANDY   What is your plan?

GRASS   I don't qualify for welfare. My parents—no. Maybe your parents?

ANDY   No. They're still pissed at what you did the last time.

GRASS   So, I don't know.

ANDY   It's getting cold out there, you need a plan.

GRASS   It's LA—it's not that cold.

ANDY   You know what I mean.

GRASS   It's not like I'm gonna freeze, it's not Chicago, not Siberia—

ANDY   When you decided to come here, what was your plan?

GRASS   Honestly? To say whatever I needed to say to get you to lend me some money.

(*A beat.*)

ANDY   You are out of options, so these are my terms. You bring me three completed job applications—that gets you a night at my house. Three applications for every night that you want to stay. You get me proof that you show up to your court dates on time, I'll feed you too.

GRASS   Andy—

ANDY   And if you get me three great songs, demos, I will listen to them. And I will give you notes. And I will call you out on being a superficial, selfish, wasteful, self-absorbed, narcissistic, infuriating, idiot at every turn.

GRASS   You mean in my songwriting—

ANDY   And we will stay in touch. I will get you a phone—and you will work until you get yourself right and you will call me three times a day if I say so. If you don't do that, if you find a way to flake out, you're in the cold. And you damn well won't be able to blame me.

GRASS   Can I think about it?

ANDY   No.

GRASS   No?

ANDY   No.

GRASS   Okay.

ANDY   Okay?

GRASS   Okay. Yes. You've got a deal.

(*A beat.*)

(*The lights shift.*)

END OF PLAY

THE HARVEST BALL

Susan Goodell

Harvest Ball premiered June 1–5, 2011, at Grasso's Magic Theatre, Philadelphia, produced by Crack the Glass Theatre Company. It was directed by Polly Rose Edelstein.

The cast:
IDA: Tiffany Brink
FAYE: Stephanie King

CHARACTERS

IDA: Polite southern young lady, 20s to 30s.
FAYE: Another polite young lady, 20s to 30s.

TIME

The 1950s, in actuality or as lived by the characters' social group.

SETTING

Tea time in IDA's formally decorated dining room.

———————

(FAYE *and* IDA, *both in dresses, are sharing a formal-looking arrangement of tea and cookies.* IDA *tries to ply* FAYE *with another cookie.*)

IDA   Take another. Come on. No one makes sugar cookies like I do . . . though I hate to brag.

FAYE   I never can resist your cookies. Say, what did you put in this tea?

IDA   Apricot preserves. You can never make tea too sweet, that's my rule. So. You got your dress for the Harvest Ball yet?

FAYE   Just started looking.

IDA   Louise says she's going strapless this year. Makes me almost glad I'm not going. Least I don't have to see Louise strapless.

FAYE   Oh Ida. Someone might still ask you.

IDA   So you know my question.

FAYE   Now, Ida, Don't ask.

IDA   Come on, you have to tell me.

FAYE   Stop thinking about, talking about asking about Raymond. It only hurts you to—

IDA   Hurt me. I need to know the truth.

FAYE   OK. He's taking her.

IDA   Oh God, why did you tell me that? What in the world can he see in Clara? You know he likes me more—

FAYE   Will you listen? You know Raymond is engaged to Clara.

IDA   That isn't right; and if it is, she tricked him into it. Surface things. That's what Raymond sees in Clara.

FAYE   Ida, I am saying this—God's truth—as your friend. But shouldn't you be discouraged after all this time chasing Raymond? You've been trying to get a date with him since 7th grade.

IDA   It's not chasing when two people would be right together. Even you said Raymond and I would be right together.

FAYE   When did I say that?

IDA   Seventh grade. We agreed. I'd marry your cousin and you'd marry mine. We'd be in each others' families.

FAYE   We also wondered how we could be sisters, Ida, but we know now that's impossible.

IDA   You got your part of the bargain. You did marry my cousin.

FAYE   Elwin loved me.

IDA   Though he didn't know it 'til I helped you, and it's your turn to help me.

FAYE   I know what you're asking and I won't do it.

IDA   I'm not asking you to kill her. It's only temporary nausea.

FAYE   It's still not right. And you've had this crazy idea since 7th grade. (*Screams and grabs abdomen.*) Ohhh. Ohhh. What! What!

IDA   So you'll help me, won't you?

FAYE   (*Wailing.*) No. No. OWWWWW. WHAT DID YOU DO!

IDA   I put ground elderberry roots in your tea.

FAYE   Ohhh Ohhh.

IDA   See. You're fine. You're not dead. Just before the Harvest Ball give Clara a little elderberry root, she'll stay home, Raymond will ask me and everything will be beautiful. If you promise to give elderberry root to Clara, I'll give you the antidote right now.

FAYE   I will not. I have principles Ida.

IDA   (*Screams.*) Ohhhhh! Ohhhh!

FAYE   Oh God. It works.

IDA   Ohhhh. Ohhhh. What works?

FAYE   Don't worry. Ohhh. She said it wouldn't kill you.

IDA   Ohhhh. Noooooo. What did you do?

FAYE   I promised, ohhh. Clara ohhhh, I'd get you out of the . . . way. Ahh. She's tired of you chasing Raymond.

IDA   Ohhhh. I'm not chasing Raymond. Ohhhh. What did you give me?

FAYE   Wisteria seeds.

IDA   You shouldn't do that. Uhhhh. Is there even an antidote for wisteria seeds?

FAYE   Oh, don't worry.

IDA   Ow. See what I'm talking about? Ow. Clara is really mean.

FAYE   I didn't want to do it. She made me.

IDA   Ohhh. So I'll give you the antidote if you give me the antidote.

FAYE   (*Still affected.*) Uh-huh. Uh-huh. Promise you won't tell Clara.

IDA   Are you kidding?

(*Both women take bottles out of their handbags, exchange and drink, giving them sweet relief.*)

FAYE   You'll feel fine soon. Wisteria seeds are really mild, for a poison.

IDA   That's good. Faye?

FAYE   Uh?

IDA   This reminds me of the time we got rid of Dixie so you could go to the Harvest Ball with Elwin.

FAYE   We did it for an important cause. Elwin and I were right for each other. I married Elwin. Ida, come on. I'm not going to poison Clara. She's too dangerous, so don't ask again.

IDA   I'm going to wither up and die. Raymond was the last single man left in town.

FAYE   No he isn't. What about Sam?

IDA   Oh . . . yeah . . . Sam. Forgot about Sam. Maybe 'cause Sam . . . never gave me the time of day.

FAYE   Sam . . . never gave you the time of day cause you always chased Raymond.

IDA   I don't chase Raymond.

FAYE   The whole town knows you're chasing Raymond.

IDA   That isn't true, and it's humiliating.

FAYE   Fact: Sam wanted to take you to the Harvest Ball, but the only way he'd have a chance was to poison Raymond, which he won't do.

IDA   Sam, really said he'd take me to the Harvest Ball? Ohhh. When does this stuff wear off?

FAYE   Should I tell Sam you'd go to the Harvest Ball, if he asks you?

IDA   If he asks me and Raymond hasn't broken up with Clara I could go with Sam.

FAYE   OK. You know Sam is my cousin. (IDA *is puzzled*.) You can have more than one cousin.

IDA   Really? Sam is your cousin? So if things work out with Sam I could we could be like . . . .

FAYE AND IDA   Almost sisters.

FAYE   See? Just like we always talked about.

IDA   I hope this works out Faye. Want another sugar cookie?

FAYE   I'll take another cookie. But no more tea.

IDA   We'll have to throw out the tea. It was good though. (*She sighs*.) Isn't the Harvest Ball the most beautiful event all year?

FAYE   It sure is.

(*Curtain*.)

END OF PLAY

HUNGRY, HUNGRY HIPPO BURGERS

Scot Walker

CHARACTERS

MARILU: 16-18, cashier at Hungry Hungry Hippo Burger. An energetic female with a Type-A personality. She's very outgoing, persuasive, and friendly, but always gets her way (*channel Lucy from* Peanuts.)

BOB: 14-18, customer. He's wimpy, shy, and wishy-washy and easily persuaded, a lone sheep in a wolf's world.

TIME

The present.

SETTING

Hungry Hungry Hippo Burgers, a trendy hamburger joint.

NOTES

MARILU has an iPad or tablet. A bare stage with one table or rostrum dividing MARILU from BOB. The jingle is sung to the tune of *The William Tell Overture* (the *Lone Ranger* theme song.)

(MARILU *is fingering her iPad and gloriously singing the last few words of the Hungry Hungry Hippo jingle until* BOB *fidgets, clearing his throat and finally gets her attention.*)

MARILU   (*Singing.*) Give me a hip, give me a hip, give me a hip, hip, hip, give me a Hip. . .po hamburger. (*Speaking.*) Welcome to Hungry Hungry Hippo Burgers, how may I help you?

BOB   I'll take a hamburger, fries, and a chocolate shake, please.

MARILU   That will be $5.69, plus sixty-two cents tax, plus nine cents for the insurance for a total of (*Punches iPad.*).

BOB   Insurance?

MARILU   Six forty.

BOB   Why do I need insurance?

MARILU   (*Reading from IPad.*) For today and today only you can insure your entire meal for a mere nine cents—that's just three cents per item.

BOB   What is it with this insurance . . . thingy? All I want is a quick lunch, but I keep thinking about that sweet Hungry, Hungry Hippo jingle and—

MARILU   (*Singing a jingle to the tune of* The William Tell Overture.) Give me a hip, give me a hip, give me a hip, hip, hip, give me a hip, give me a hip, give me a hip, hip, hip, give me a hip, give me a hip, give me a hip, hip, hip, give me a HIP. . . PO—

MARILU AND BOB   (*Singing together in harmony.*) Ham-burger!

MARILU   So which will it be? Soda or shake?

BOB   Shake, no . . . soda . . . no, give me a shake. Yes . . . the shake, not the soda, the shake.

MARILU   (*Visually pissed, motioning with her hands for* BOB *to hurry along with his decision.*) Not the shake, I already got that . . . which insurance plan?

BOB   Insurance for what? Choking to death on a Hungry Hungry Hippo Burger?

MARILU   Exactly!

BOB   You're kidding me!

MARILU   Nope.

BOB   You're not kidding me?

MARILU   Nope. A Hungry Hungry Hippo Burger is your best choice for a fine meal with great ambience and full medical coverage. Consider it Obamacare for the fast and hungry. Here, read this (*Shoves iPad across the counter.*)

BOB   (*Tapping his fingers on the counter in mild agitation.*) I barely have time to eat, let alone read! (*Pushes iPad back to* MARILU.)

MARILU   (*Reading from iPad.*) Yes, I understand. You said, you barely have time to enjoy our fine food, let alone read about the benefits of insurance coverage. Is that right?

BOB   (*Coldly.*) Yes.

MARILU   (*Turns page after page on iPad, then reads.*) "I can understand your frustration sir or madam."

BOB   I am a "Sir."

MARILU   (*Looking up.*) Yes, sir, I'm sorry. I get carried away reading these directives sometimes. (MARILU *flips through the iPad looking for her place.*) There's so much marvelous wisdom here! It's like listening to Rush Limbaugh! Everything he says is totally off the wall just like these directives and the more I try to understand, the less I do! Oh well, I'm sure it'll make sense in time! (*Finds her place on the iPad.*) Ah, here it is. Let me quote, "We at Triple HB." (*Pauses, trying to interpret the meaning of the letters, and then in an epiphany shouts.*) Triple HB! Wow. Now I get it. That stands for Hungry Hungry Hippo Burgers! (*Prances around the room.*) That's so cool. See, I was right. It is like listening to Rush Limbaugh . . . or Donald Trump, everything they say sounds like nonsense . . . but there is meaning there . . . isn't there? (*Doesn't wait for an answer; grins, mutters.*)

(*Flips through the iPad, motions for BOB to follow along as she moves to his side and has him read along following her finger.*)

MARILU AND BOB   (*together, reading.*) Triple HB has developed a unique opportunity to improve the quality of health for all our patrons and avoid calamity—

BOB   (*Piqued.*) There's gonna be a calamity if I don't get my Hippo Burger. (*He kicks his foot petulantly, boyishly.*)

MARILU   Put your thumbprint here and I'll get things rolling: your Hungry Hippy low-cost term insurance will come right up. (*Slides iPad to* BOB, *slightly antsy but badgering him for the sale.*) You can put your thumbprint there. (*Shows where to thumb the pad and then holds* *both her thumbs up grinning like a monkey.*) Like this. (MARILU *demonstrates, placing her thumb on the iPad.*) Like this. (*She shows him again.*) Presto—like it's magic! (*Thumbing once more.*) Like this, okay? Come on, (*Sweetly.*) be a happy hippo!

BOB   (*Loudly.*) I AM NOT a happy damned Hippo!

MARILU   Sir, do not raise your voice at me! This is not your average watering hole—this is a sacred hippo haven!

BOB   (*Meekly.*) May I please have my hamburger.

MARILU   Certainly! (*Types on the iPad while humming "give me a hip, give me a hip, give me a hip, hip, hip."*) Your policy covers deaths due to burps, belches and farts! (*Embarrassed.*) Oh my! I didn't know we went that far. That's nasty.

BOB   I decline. I decline, okay? I don't want the freaking insurance. Just give me my burger!

MARILU   (*Loudly.*) SIR, Nobody WANTS insurance. (*Flips through the iPad and reads in a normal voice.*) "You agree, don't you, that we all need burp, belch, choke, and fart insurance? Picture yourself dead, picture your children fatherless." How many children do you have, sir?

BOB   What do children have to do with a Hippo Burger? (*Pause.*) I'm single and after spending time with you, I'm staying single . . . FOREVER. (*Quickly turns around, then walks back.*) And stop calling me "sir," okay? I'm Bob, just call me Bob, and for God's sakes stop bobbing me along—just give me my burger, toss it on a damn tray, point me at a table, and let me eat in peace. Is that possible?

MARILU   Don't be mean, Bob. I wasn't mean to you, was I, Bob? (*Reading.*) "The small investment on your Hungry Hungry Hippo Burger will only cost nine cents, unless you want cheese, and then you get the . . ." Oh, my gosh! You're not going to believe this, but if you get the burger without fries, you get the insurance free.

BOB   I don't want the insurance!

MARILU No one wants insurance—even though it's the best way to ensure our customers' health and safety for as long as they remain eating here at the Hippo.

BOB What? That's it? The insurance covers my health as long as I'm eating. What if I choke to death after I leave or . . . or I fart myself to death?

MARILU BOB, as long as you still have food in your mouth or on your tray, you're covered.

BOB Okay, wrap it up, I'll sign. (*Pause.*) Has anyone ever died here and collected this insurance thingy?

MARILU Thumbprint here. (BOB *thumbs.*) A man choked to death right over there—and his heirs collected ten million dollars. (*Takes back iPad, pushes a button to order his food.*) Food will be right up faster than a hippo belches. His heirs are mourning his death in the South Pacific.

BOB Why the South Pacific?

MARILU No idea.

BOB (*Beat, drumming fingers on counter, thinking.*) Hey, do you see that guy eating over there? Did he buy insurance?

MARILU No, as a matter of fact. (*Mutters.*) He was as stubborn and bull headed as—

BOB Good, in addition to my lunch, I'll take out an insurance policy on him.

MARILU Wow! Awesome! That will be nine cents, Bob, thumbprint please! (*She slides the iPad to* BOB.)

(BOB *thumbs and walks over to the "man."* BOB *then acts out choking the man to death, including gloriously loud sound effects.*)

BOB Bali! The South Sea island is Bali. Do you know Bali doesn't allow extradition? If you commit a crime in the USA and move to Bali, our government is powerless to prosecute you! (*Pause.*) So, have your company wire me the money to General Delivery, Bali. (*Sings loudly.*) Give me a hip, give me a hip, give me a hip, hip, hip, give me a BALI hamburger!

 END OF PLAY

HUNTER'S SUMMARY

Max Baker

CHARACTERS

KIP: M or F, any ethnicity, any age.
HUNTER: M, any ethnicity, any age.

These two characters live together but are desperately mismatched from a casual visual perspective.

TIME

Present.

SETTING

The cereal aisle in a labyrinthine discount superstore.

NOTE

KIP may wear shiny gold shorts, dress socks, sandals, and an American Eagle T-shirt, and have wild hair.

HUNTER may have on a scuba mask and nozzle, camouflage pants, boots, or other items he may have picked up in today's shopping trip.

In the cart: A small flat-screen TV in box, a lampshade, some brightly colored polo shirts, toilet paper, hamburger buns, mop, dog food, and a Wiffle ball and bat.

———————

Lights

(KIP *is pushing the cart, looking for cereal, followed by* HUNTER, *talking.*)

HUNTER   . . . so it starts, see it starts
wait, I don't remember how it starts—it just begins
and there's this guy whose like—he's sorta a boss guy—
and he's always on the phone with *his* boss—
the real head guy, only you never see him, and his wife
the guy's wife, the main guy, his wife
you see her
she's at home cooking dinner and doesn't know about all the
stuff the guy has to deal with all day long, the main guy
coz all these problems start happening and

—that's right—it starts in a church
or I guess it's a church, there's this cross and he's praying or
    something
you know when you're on your knees and looking up at a crucifix

KIP   (*Reading cereal box.*) Inside this box: One Door Knocker from
Monster Cereals.

HUNTER   You know who's in it?
That funny guy who was in that other film with—you know—
about how he's in Hawaii with his girlfriend
only she wasn't supposed to be there and she shows up
and they go surfboarding
He's in it, only not very much, and the girl who was—what's her
    name—she was in
that one where they're trying to escape being killed by clones or
    robots or—they're on a spaceship—
or it's earth but not
and there's two of her, only one of them is a clone and she doesn't
    know it
with whatshisname, the Scottish dude, and they fall off the building
    and everyone's after them
Remember that film?
Anyway she's in it

KIP   (*Reading cereal box.*) What Makes Cap'n Crunch So Much Fun?

HUNTER   and there's another girl, at the beginning of this film, the
    one you've got to see
and someone's taking photographs of her and the cops show up
and then there's this other little guy who's in the desert, or a ranch
    or someplace
and he gets recruited by the main guy to be like a—a—a—a—
what's that film where there's a fire and a staircase and he's wearing
    a hat?

KIP   Crisp whole wheat and bran flakes
with delicious nut-covered raisins and slivered almonds

HUNTER   Anyway the main guy wants that guy to be like the dude
in that film.

KIP   Free Schwinn decals, set of three, with $1 S and H.
See side panel for nutritional facts.

HUNTER   So this cowboy guy gets all dressed up and goes to a
    cocktail party
and—oh—yeah, see one of the guys that the main guy is supposed
    to be looking after is missing,
and this other woman kinda knows about it, or
I didn't get that part coz she had a sister and they looked the same
so that part was hard to follow only later you find out he's part of
    this gang and they
play chess or it's a group, a meeting
only he doesn't know what they're meeting about
and then the main guy talks to the cowboy guy about
finding the other guy that was a funny scene
Plus he has to go on a date with a Mexican woman and . . .

KIP   Organic Wild Puffs

HUNTER   oh yeah—there's this scene on a boat
and they've got a suitcase of money and oh! One scene, there's this
    one bit where there's all these people standing around and this
    one guy has a clipboard and is calling people's names and
is trying to get answers out of everyone, that made me laugh

KIP   Wheat Free No Trans Fat
Fruity Punch Crunchy Corn and Oat Cereal USDA Organic
Excellent Source of 11 Essential Vitamins and Minerals

HUNTER   Man you gotta see it, you have to see it.

KIP   May Reduce the Risk of Heart Disease.

HUNTER   So anyway, in the end
oh wait before that there's this other part when the main guy talks
    to all these people who all have different points of view about
    George Clooney

That's not his name in the film, but that's who they're talking about
and one of them is saying "George Clooney is the shit"
then someone else is "No George Clooney is too old"
He isn't the main guy, George Clooney, he's the guy who ends up
    playing chess
the main guy is I don't know his name
Desiree told me he was in something I've never seen where
    supposedly he gets chased around by a crazy-looking big headed
    dude with a cattle prod
something

KIP   Get Free Milk Instantly when you buy four.

(KIP *loads big cereal boxes into the cart.*)

HUNTER   Oh, so the ending, right, right. The ending is sudden and
    and
That's right he gets offered a job by someone in a Chinese
    restaurant
and his wife thinks he should take that job
and he goes back to work the next day to his desk and picks up the
    phone and then it just ends like that
Blackout
Oh, no, wait, that's not how it ends
I mean it ends with a blackout all of a sudden, so you don't know it's
    coming
but there's another bit before that where he's trying to figure out if
    he did everything the way he was supposed to or if he's a total
    loser and he gets this look on his face
like he doesn't know or he does know but you don't know
and it's this amazing moment and then it ends. Just boom. Sudden.
    End. Out.
That's it.

(*Blackout.*)

END OF PLAY

I AM A GUN AND
I KILL PEOPLE

Erik Christian Hanson

CHARACTERS

GUN: Any gender, any race, middle-aged.
SECRETARY (BERNADETTE): 48, female, full-figured, one with a talent for gab and multitasking.
REGGIE: 64, male, front desk security, pleasant demeanor, incompetent.
CHEERLEADER: 16, female, snarky.
DISPATCHER: Mid-30s, male or female.
FEMALE COUPLE: 17, consumed by their cell phones.
PERKY GIRL: Female, 16, bespectacled.
VARIOUS STUDENTS: Mixed ages (14–17) and races.

TIME

Today or tomorrow.

SETTING

A high school like all the others. Anywhere USA.

(*Spotlight on* GUN. *It regards us for a lengthy silence, smiles, and then says all of this:*)

GUN   I am a Bushmaster XM15-E2S rifle and I kill people. It doesn't matter who holds me. It doesn't matter who fires me. I am an unstoppable force. I am very accurate from 25 yards away. I can let off 30 round magazines at will. So what if I might malfunction after 1,000 rounds?

(*Lights up to reveal the lobby of a high school.*)

Ooh, a school.

(*With a hockey equipment bag wrapped around its shoulder,* GUN *approaches* REGGIE, *an elderly man, at the check-in desk.*)

First line of defense is this guy. Are they serious?

REGGIE   You have your late slip?

(*A* CHEERLEADER *walks past him.*)

I need your late slip.

GUN He can't even slow down a snarky teen and he's going to stop me? Prevent me from getting in here and doing whatever I like? I. Don't. Think. So. (*Pauses.*) This school district should be ashamed of itself. At least get a DARE Officer.

(*A* FEMALE COUPLE *passes by.*)

REGGIE No cell phones.
   (FEMALE COUPLE *laughs.*)
   I said, "No cell phones!"

GUN His incompetence is frightening. If I'm frightened, you should be too. He's protecting your children. You'll put yourself into bed tonight thinking that this guy's the anomaly. But he's the norm. He is. Trust me on this one. Guys like him are dime a dozen in most schools across the United States. Men who get walked over by words and silence. Think he'd get walked over by me? What's he going to do, use his book of crosswords as a bulletproof vest?

(GUN *heads for the main office.*)

REGGIE Sir, excuse me, Sir?

GUN Me?

REGGIE You.

GUN What's up?

REGGIE You can't waltz right in there.

GUN I'm just dropping off my son's hockey equipment.
   (REGGIE *pauses.*)
   See him stalling? He wants to ask me for my ID. I'd give it to him, but it's not going to prevent me from getting into that office. I'll give him my wallet if he wants it.

REGGIE Go on in.

GUN And like that, I'm in the main office. It's that simple sometimes.

(GUN *approaches a full-figured* SECRETARY.)

SECRETARY   (*On phone.*) Stonington Valley School, Bernadette speaking. Chicken fajita and potato wedges. You're welcome. (*Clicks, then answers.*) Stonington Valley School, Bernadette speaking. He needs a check with the form. With the form. Yes. Uh huh. Yep. It's that or no yearbook. (*Clicks, then answers.*) Stonington Valley School, Bernadette speaking. Mrs. Burns is in a PPT at the moment. Care to try her later? Yes? No? Or hang up on me. (*Clicks, then answers.*) Stonington Valley School. Bernadette speaking.

GUN   Look at her go on that phone!

SECRETARY   (*On phone.*) Stonington Valley School, Bernadette speaking. No, it's the wrong paper. The size doesn't fit our machines. We need 8 1/2 by 11. I don't know why your order says that. Send the right paper, please. ASAP.

GUN   Poor woman is bombarded with calls like this every single day. Think it would take long to take her out? Think about it. I mean, really think about it. Now I know what's on your mind. You're wondering how long it would take Bernadette to hear me taking out Reggie. Well, I wouldn't take Reggie out first. That would be a mistake. Minor but a mistake all the same. Taking him out tips off people in the main office. Hey, Bernadette.

SECRETARY   Yes?

GUN   Do you have an emergency button behind that desk?

SECRETARY   I do.

GUN   Is it within reach?

SECRETARY   Perfectly within reach.

GUN   Listen to her. Happy about a safety button. How stupid. How tragic. This is whom I would take out first.

SECRETARY   (*On phone.*) Stonington Valley School. Bernadette speaking. Hello? Hello?

GUN   That was me who called her. (*Laughs, then:*) Bernadette?

SECRETARY   (*On phone.*) Stonington Valley School. Bernadette speaking. The prom theme is *The Great Gatsby*. Don't blame me. The students voted for it.

GUN   Oh, Bernadette?

SECRETARY   Kind of on the phone.

GUN   I see that. Just wanted you to know that you'd be my first.

SECRETARY   Wonderful.

GUN   She's so oblivious. God bless that phone.

SECRETARY   (*On phone.*) Stonington Valley School. Bernadette speaking. Mrs. Burns is still in her PPT. I would try back later. Much later.

GUN   And yes, there might be other people in this office. Kids with notes. Teachers making copies. A PPT taking place in a nearby conference room. Wouldn't matter one bit. Everyone in here would be dead in less than a minute. Dare I say, everyone in here would be dead in less than thirty seconds.

(GUN *leaves the main office, and makes its way through the hallway.*)

On I'd go through the halls . . . .

(*A bell rings. Random students walk by.*)

He'd be dead. She'd be dead. Him. Her. Him. Him. Him. Her. Her. Him. Him. Him. Him and her.

(*The hallway becomes empty.*)

And I'm assuming by this time that someone would have alerted the cops.

(*Spotlight on* DISPATCHER.)

DISPATCHER   911, what's your emergency?

(*Lights off* DISPATCHER.)

GUN   But on I'd go because it would still take the cops a few minutes. Their station is seven minutes away. Seven when the traffic is favorable. When it's not favorable, it can take as long as twelve.

Seven to twelve minutes of killing. Seven's a lot of time. Twelve's an eternity. Excuse me, I'm parched.

(GUN *makes a stop at the water fountain.*)

Most of the rooms would be locked by now. They do that. Go into lockdown mode. Sadly for them, a majority of the doors have a rectangular window on them. Sure, the teachers are told to cover them with black construction paper. They're supposed to feel good about this because I—or someone like me—couldn't see into the room. Who needs to see into the room when I can shoot through the window and open the door? (*Laughs.*) Just saying. Just saying. So, whether it was seven minutes for the cops or twelve, I would have wreaked my havoc on . . .

(*A* PERKY GIRL *with glasses walks by.* GUN *stops her.*)

Say, what's the name of this place again?

PERKY GIRL   You kidding?

GUN   Nope.

PERKY GIRL   Stonington Valley School.

GUN   I would have wreaked my havoc on Stonington Valley because I am a Bushmaster XM15-E2S rifle and I kill people.

(*Lights dim as* GUN *surveys the surroundings and laughs at all the potential damage it could do.*)

(*Blackout.*)

END OF PLAY

THE ITEMS FORGOTTEN

Tara Meddaugh

CHARACTERS

KIRA: A woman in her 20s–40s. She is married to Travis.
TRAVIS: A man in his 20s–50s. He is married to Kira.

TIME

Present.

SETTING

Outside of Kira and Travis's house. On their porch or thereabouts. It is winter, cold.

———————————

(*At rise:* KIRA *and her husband* TRAVIS *are searching around their front porch. It is winter, cold.* KIRA *holds up a fake rock/hidden key holder.*)

KIRA   They were right here last time.

TRAVIS   Well, they're not there now.

KIRA   I can see that.

TRAVIS   So?

KIRA   Are you blaming me for this? Are you seriously doing that?

TRAVIS   You're the last one who used them.

KIRA   I told you—I told you, specifically, to make sure to put them back in the rock! Where we always put them!

TRAVIS   I didn't get them out.

KIRA   But I asked you to put them back!

(*Puts the key rock down.*)

TRAVIS   I can't keep track of you. Honestly, Kira, I can't keep track of every single thing you do.

KIRA   I didn't do anything—I just asked—

TRAVIS   I can't keep track of everything you ask me to do then. You're like a drill sergeant.

KIRA   It's the only way you do things.

TRAVIS   It's not the only way I do things. You think you're, what, the Siri of my life? I need you for every single step I take?

KIRA   Travis—

TRAVIS   I go to work, don't I? I get there on my own.

KIRA   I have to wake you up because you ignore the alarm.

TRAVIS   Do you write lesson plans for me? Do you go on interviews for me?

KIRA   I help you get prepared for them.

TRAVIS   Okay, well.

KIRA   I'm just saying—you need direction. Otherwise you just—I don't know—it's so cold—I don't know, you just run in place or something.

TRAVIS   (*Shakes head.*) That's what you think.

KIRA   It's what I see—having been married to you for 7 years. I don't like having to tell you what to do every day, but if I don't—

TRAVIS   I'll what?

KIRA   You'll—

TRAVIS   Will I sleep in a pile of trash because you don't tell me to take it out?

KIRA   I honestly don't know.

TRAVIS   Oh, come on, Kira. Come on. This whole thing—you're just—you can't admit you messed up. And this isn't the first time.

(*Pause.*)

KIRA   I thought they were in my pocket.

(*Pause.*)

TRAVIS   I know you did. It was an accident.

KIRA It was.

TRAVIS Of course it was.

(*He takes his gloves off and gives them to her.*)

KIRA You're not cold?

TRAVIS You're colder, I'm sure. And those gloves you wear—I keep telling you to get warmer ones. Those are so thin.

KIRA I have to be able to help buckle Jack in.

TRAVIS Okay, well. You don't have to do that right now.

KIRA (*Puts gloves on.*) It's the third time this week I've locked myself out.

TRAVIS I know.

(*Pause.*)

KIRA I just have so much going on in my head.

TRAVIS I know.

KIRA With my mom—

TRAVIS You're an amazing daughter helping her like this.

KIRA I don't know how long she can stay at her house.

(*Pause.*)

TRAVIS We'll cross that bridge when we come to it.

(*Pause.*)

KIRA Do you think I'm getting Alzheimer's too?

TRAVIS No.

KIRA Are you sure?

TRAVIS Forgetting your keys because you're overwhelmed does not mean you have Alzheimer's.

(*Pause.*)

KIRA   I forgot to pick up Jack from preschool yesterday too.

TRAVIS   You didn't tell me that.

KIRA   I was going to. I just . . . they called me. So, I mean, he was safe. He was fine. He got to play *Zingo* with one of the teachers. He didn't think anything of it, but . . . I just . . . I can't believe I forgot.

TRAVIS   Why'd you forget? What were you doing?

KIRA   Nothing. Really—I wasn't sleeping. I wasn't at my mom's house, or at the gym or engrossed in—in—anything! I was just . . . I don't know. I was just vacuuming, I think. And then . . . it was three, and . . . I saw the clock, but it didn't—it didn't register to me. Isn't that weird?

TRAVIS   Hm.

(*Pause.*)

Maybe you should see someone.

KIRA   A therapist?

TRAVIS   Maybe.

(*Pause.*)

KIRA   I do have a lot on my plate.

TRAVIS   And maybe just—just let me handle myself for now. I can do that. I managed a few decades before I met you. You make me better, Kira—you do. I know that; everyone knows that. But I can—I can remember to put the milk away after I have coffee, and I can schedule an oil change for the car. You don't need to tell me every step of the way.

(*Pause.*)

KIRA   Okay.

(*Pause.*)

I'll try.

(*Pause.*)

TRAVIS   And I'm sorry I didn't put the keys back in the rock when you asked.

KIRA   It's okay.

(*Pause.*)

It's—I'm . . . .

TRAVIS   It's okay. We're . . . we're on—(*the same team*).

KIRA   The same team.

(*Pause.*)

TRAVIS   Yes, we are.

(*Pause.*)

And our team is locked out right now. I guess I'll have to—break a window or something? Call the alarm company? I wish I could jimmy open a door with a credit card. Something my dad never taught me.

(HE *starts to walk around back.*)

KIRA   Jack's bedroom window isn't locked!

TRAVIS   It's not?

KIRA   He wanted to feel the rain this morning when he got up, so I opened it. I was going to lock it back up—I always lock it, but—I forgot to this morning, I guess.

TRAVIS   I'll get the ladder from the garage! See, Kira?

(HE *kisses her.*)

What would I do without you?

(HE *runs to the garage to get a ladder.*)

(KIRA *sits on the steps and looks off.*)

 END OF PLAY

I WANT TO MIND-READ YOU ALL NIGHT

Catherine Weingarten

Original production information: Ohio University Midnight Madness, "Super Power" Madness produced by Philana Omorotionmwan, through Ohio University's MFA Playwriting weekly short play fest. Original cast included Ben Stockman and Ellie Clark. Directed by Catherine Weingarten. February 5th, 2016, in the Hahne Theater in Ohio University, Athens, Ohio.

CHARACTERS

PIPPA: Late 20s/early 30s, loves baking cakes with her and her BF's faces on them; she's sweet, maybe a little repressed, and has an intense otherworldly connection with DALTON.

DALTON: Late 20s/early 30s, mailman, super earnest, wishes he was a poet but it's not gonna happen; has an intense otherworldly connection with PIPPA.

TIME

The present.

SETTING

Characters' thoughts/open space.

——————————

(PIPPA *and* DALTON *face the audience and address them.*)

DALTON   I don't know how it happened, ya know

PIPPA   We're like a really cute couple ya knowwwww,
Cause like . . .
When I *tell Dalton*
We should wear matching couples overalls
For our Tuesday-Afternoonnn-Picnic-Date, he says Yes!
And he wears *whatever* color hat I need him to!
And that's important to me,
(Cause like it should be, right?)

PIPPA/DALTON   I can tell we're just the best couple
Cause like we can just sit together like
On Pippa's bedsheets with pictures of my face she custom designed
On the Internet
And she'll like . . .
This is gunna sound weirdd :/

PIPPA   I just know what he's *thinking* all the time,
Like he'll be looking at extra chunnnky peanut butter

(And to most girls that wouldn't matter,)
Like they would just assume their bf is spacing out
And not take notice
But I fricking NOTICE, ya know?
Like notice *hard* and I can tell what he's thinking about
When he was 10 and his dad said
He wasn't *cool* enough to wear a fedora,
That really *hurt* him.

DALTON   Like she knows what I'm thinking and like
I can do it *too* cause like were so *into*
Each other and stuff like they should have a fricking parade
Dedicated to us like as a couple cause like
When we look at each other purple fireworks go off
And like celebrity couples get divorced—just thinking about
How into each other *we are*—

PIPPA   I know he loves me cause like
I literally know it.
Like he thinks about it all the time
Sometimes it kindaa gets boring—

DALTON   God I love her,
Her lips taste like chocolate-covered strawberries dipped
In sprinkles and cocaine!
I shudder and kinda freak out just tasting them,
(but like in a good way ☺)

PIPPA   When he touches my face, his hands feel like oak:
Like so thick and hard
And reassuring, like the most reassuring
Hands could ever even be or want to be.

(DALTON *and* PIPPA *get more stoner friendly.*)

DALTON   She has the most beautiful dreams,
Like once she dreamed we were both
Birds and like we
Flew all over the sky which was for some reason

Bright purple
And we just needed each other so bad
And were so into each other we couldn't even pay attention
And we like flew into the stars and planes
And like it didn't even hurt that much cause we were so into each
    other,
She forgot it when she woke up, but I didn't.
I don't know what I would do if I couldn't listen to her dreams.

PIPPA   He has the most interesting dreams,
He tells me he dreams about me
Crawling on a beach in a bikini made of fire
Whispering my name.
But I know he really dreams about
Playing Clue with his grandma,
Like so cute and innocent right?
And like sometimes I'm so close
To his dreams, I can just swim right in them,
We're like *so* close.

DALTON   She has a lot of dreams about me . . . like "kinkier" ones
When we're like doing it
And my body is like Superman friendly
Like thick like slab of meat
And my voice is different like lower
And I wink a lot, and is it really me
If everything about me is different?
Like what's that supposed to mean?

PIPPA   (*Getting pissed.*)
I don't think he likes my dreams cause
When I wake up
He sometimes glare at me :/
It's just like *other couples*
Don't have to deal with this, they can just
Not know stuff and be fine.
They can just like say they love each other

But think whatever they want—

(*Pace gets more desperate.*)

DALTON   I don't really know how it started and stuff,
But I can feel like her moving away from me.
She has these thoughts about me
Moving to China for mysterious reasons potentially illegal reasons
And us just forgetting about each other.
And she giggles when she thinks about that,
I don't wanna frickin' move to China!

PIPPA   Ever since I was *little*
I knew I'd be good at dating!!
Cause like I have the *face* for it and the *disposition*
And my *laugh* sounds like adorable Barbie friendly church bells!
But like I never knew it would be like this,
Like every single thought I have,
Like he can read it like a book.
Like sometimes I forget if it's my personality or his
Or my dream or his,
But like I know it'll be fine right?
Cause like people really like us as a couple and stuff
And like I'm good at dating and stuff!!
And I *bake cakes* for a living which makes me cuter ;)

DALTON   Sometimes when I'm at work, it gets bad like
I can't even focus.
Like I'll be so in-tune with her like,
I'll deliver mail to the wrong houses.
Like all I'll be thinking about
Is what color "you're the slut of the night" lipstick
Pippa wants from CVS.
But like, it's ok right??
Cause like we're *dating* and we're like meanttt
To be together and like be so in love that
We melt into each other and like lose our personality

And stuff and become *one big sweet caramel popcorn ball*
Of love ☺

DALTON/PIPPA   I don't know how it happened, ya know

PIPPA   I don't like thinking about him anymore,
I'd rather just think about cakes
With photos of me on a beach on them, like I wanna change
My thoughts or something, like put them on a cleanse
(cleanses are super in).

DALTON   We've both been having these thoughts lately
That like things aren't working and stuff,
Like and I have this feeling it's not coming back, like we're not
Gunna be anything
Anymore.
And all I can think about is I'm gunna miss her dreams,
I'm gunna miss swimming in the water
Of them and becoming a pirate for them
Or a bird, especially a bird, I'm gunna miss that so bad.

(*A look between* PIPPA *and* DALTON *that lasts two beats and then:*)

END OF PLAY

THE JOURNEY
TO THE CEDAR
FOREST

Don Nigro

Characters

BEN: Late 20s.
TRACY: Early 20s.

Time

1970s.

Setting

An attic bedroom in a cabin in the woods by a lake. All we can see when the light is on is the bed surrounded by darkness.

————————————

(BEN *and* TRACY *in bed. Night. Sound of owls. He turns on the light. She's sitting on the bed with her chin resting on her knees.*)

BEN   All right. What is it?

TRACY   The owls woke me up. I like owls. But I'm afraid of them. Because they eat mice. I like owls but I identify with the mice. Did you touch me? When I was sleeping?

BEN   Probably.

TRACY   Well, stop it. I don't like you touching me when I'm sleeping.

BEN   Yes you do.

TRACY   Don't tell me what I like. You don't know what I like.

BEN   You're trembling. Are you cold? Do you want me to go downstairs and turn up the heat?

TRACY   No. Then I'll be too hot. Besides, if my father hears you moving around in the cabin at night, he'll shoot you. He's probably been looking for an excuse to shoot you for a while now. He doesn't like you.

BEN   I don't think your father likes anybody.

TRACY   He likes owls. My father identifies with the owls. I've been cold ever since we got caught in the rain, in the woods. I've been dreaming about the woods. I dreamed I found a dead man in the woods.

BEN   Was it me?

TRACY   Maybe. But a little better looking. He told me to take off all my clothes.

BEN   A dead man was talking to you?

TRACY   It was a dream. Then we were here in the cabin. And you told me to lay down on the kitchen table.

BEN   So it was me? I was the talking dead man?

TRACY   I guess so. And I was naked, and you covered me all over with flour.

BEN   Did I butter you first?

TRACY   What the hell kind of a stupid question is that? Why would want to you butter me?

BEN   So the flour would stick. Why would you want me to pour flour all over you?

TRACY   I didn't want you to pour flour over me. Everything that happens to you in your dreams isn't something you want.

BEN   That's not what Freud says. He says—

TRACY   Oh, fuck Freud up the ass with a barge pole. You're always bringing up that Freudian bullshit. Do you want to hear the rest of this dream or not?

BEN   More than life itself.

TRACY   So I took a piece of chalk and drew a circle around myself on the kitchen table. So the demon couldn't get to me.

BEN   So first I'm a corpse, and then I pour flour all over you, and now I'm a demon.

TRACY   Who was that letter from?

BEN   What letter?

TRACY   Just before we drove up to the cabin. You got a letter and you were reading it in the car and you put it in your book.

BEN   I think this was in your dream.

TRACY   It wasn't in my dream. I saw it. You put it in that book about Gilgamesh. You read the weirdest books. Gilgamesh and Enkidu were going to this cedar forest and there was this monster there named Humbaba or something like that and he told them to stay the hell away from his trees so they cut off his head.

BEN   You actually read my book?

TRACY   I read books. I was looking for the letter. But it wasn't there.

BEN   There was no letter. You dreamed the letter.

TRACY   That's what George Brent told Merle Oberon in that movie. He was trying to drive her crazy. Confuse her about what was real. I always have bad dreams up here. Somebody touching me in the dark. Or throwing a baby down a well. Or all my dolls come alive and start jabbering at me around the bed with their eyes all glowing. And this clown taking naked pictures of me. And then somebody on top of me. I don't know if it was the clown or not. I can only remember things in fragments. My father hates you so much. He's got a gun, you know. He could kill you and bury you in the woods and nobody would ever find you.

BEN   You would. You'd find me. In your dream.

TRACY   But then it would be too late.
(*Pause.*)
If I was unfaithful to you, would you want to know?

BEN   What?

TRACY   If I was unfaithful to you, would you want to know?

BEN   I would want you not to.

TRACY   Not to tell you?

BEN   Not to be unfaithful to me.

TRACY   But everybody is.

BEN   I'm not.

TRACY   Only because you're insane.
(*Pause.*)
Well, good night.

(*She pulls the covers over herself and lies down with her back to him.*)

BEN   Wait a minute.

TRACY   I'm sleeping now. I'm asleep.

BEN   You can't ask me a question like that and then just turn over and go to sleep.

TRACY   I just did. This is me sleeping.

(*Pause.*)

BEN   Are you going away again?

TRACY   Everybody goes away.
(*Pause. Sound of owls.*)
Ben? Why did they cut down the cedar forest? In that stupid book.

BEN   To make a gate. So they could close the gate and nobody could get in and hurt them.

TRACY   But what about the owls? Where did the owls go? When they cut down all the trees?

BEN   I don't know. I don't know where owls go.

(*Pause.*)

TRACY   I wouldn't have cut down all those trees. Because once you chop it down, it's gone. You can't get it back.
(*Pause.*)
You can touch me now if you want. But only in the dark.

(*BEN looks at her. Then he turns out the light. Sound of owls.*)

END OF PLAY

KEEP BREATHING

Laurence Carr

Keep Breathing is a rewritten play from a longer work, *Trouble Down Below*, which was originally commissioned by Ohio University and produced at the Reality Theatre in Columbus, Ohio, in 1991, directed by Dennis Dalen. The longer play was produced by the Aegean Theatre in New York City in 1997, directed by Greg Paul.

CHARACTERS

Jane: 20s, a friend of Julia.
Julia: 20s, a friend of Jane.

TIME

The present.

SETTNG

Julia's apartment in an American city.

Jane is visiting her friend, Julia. They half-heartedly work through a yoga video, trying various poses (asanas) that they're watching on one of Julia's screens. The video is unseen by the audience. Gentle music plays in the background. Julia has recently been fired from a corporate job and Julia is now out of a relationship.

———————

(Jane *and* Julia *are in* Julia's *apartment watching a yoga video.*)

Julia   Son of a bitch . . . (*Beat.*) Bastard . . .

Jane   We're supposed to be focus on breathing.

Julia   I am, goddammit!

Jane   I think you're over-focusing.

Julia   I just thought of another way. I install a metal plate in the floor in front of the urinal. I electrify it. I electrify the urinal. He stands on the metal plate. He starts to piss— the circuit's complete. Ten thousand volts. He's dead.

Jane   What if he's wearing rubber soles?

Julia   I hire a shoeshine guy. Guys are always in a hurry. He takes off his shoes while he pees.

Jane   I'll never touch a guy's feet again.

Julia   I'll make it company policy. You know how guys suck up to that.

JANE With that kind of thinking I would've promoted you instead of . . .

JULIA "Fired," Jane. I was fired. The bad "F" word.

JANE Who pulled the plug?

JULIA Scotty. Sweet little Scotty. The one who was, God, I hate this phrase, "grooming me." Sounds like the Westminster fucking Dog Show. All that stuff I got for him. All the ways I got that stuff for him. And when push came to shove, he goes with Mr. Outside.

JANE The guy from Boston?

JULIA At the interview, Scotty made him coffee. Made him coffee. I should have known then.

JANE Were you seeing him?

JULIA Who, Scotty? A couple of times. Just to blow off some steam. It was—casual.

JANE Exit Julia.

JULIA And Gordon. Gordon, for chrissake, he practically ran the place. I should have faded into the woodwork the day I got there.

JANE You're not a fader.

JULIA I'd still be there.

JANE Bored to death.

JULIA Instead of scared to death.

JANE You always land on your feet. I never come in for a landing . . . .

JULIA Gordon landed on his feet. He was always tight with some headhunter at Wrightson and Todd. They snatched him up the next day. He said maybe he could use me.

JANE As what?

JULIA   Some kind of consultant. Maybe work up to . . . oh, hell, Jane, be his goddam secretary, open his mail, answer his mail.

JANE   Make his coffee . . . ? (JULIA *is silent.*) Are you sleeping with him?

JULIA   No. I like him. I like—liked—working with him. It's all so weird.

JANE   Did you ever sleep with Matt?

JULIA   Somebody would have murdered somebody.

JANE   Not even before? Back in college?

JULIA   (*Beat.*) Are you seeing him again?

JANE   No. I just . . . wondered . . .

JULIA   You deserve better.

JANE   We were a car crash. Twisted metal and a ball of flame.

JULIA   Wow. My ex just stopped calling. He's just an amorphous blob now.

JANE   I want to forget everything. Do you remember things?

JULIA   I remember him painting my legs—we were . . . never mind. (*Takes a big inhale and exhale.*) Gone.

JANE   Did he make you happy? Did it work?

JULIA   "He" or "It"? Ahhh, the Holy Grail.

JANE   Did he . . . was he attentive?

JULIA   Oh, smooth. Very smooth. He'd always catch me at a weak moment.

JANE   They follow the herd, waiting for a weak moment. We keep forgetting it's the lioness who does the hunting.

JULIA   Yeah, but the lion gets all the press. It's that hair. (*Pause.*) We don't need jerks beating us up.

JANE   He beat you?

JULIA   No— No. Things just got a little out of hand. It was a stupid mistake.

JANE   I'm sorry.

JULIA   For what?

JANE   I don't know. Everything. It's nice here. Quiet.

JULIA   Too quiet?

JANE   No. Quiet like— after great sex. Or even OK sex. Don't they say that?

JULIA   File under fiction.

JANE   All I want is a small, clean room.

JULIA   Try the convent?

JANE   My room at Jenna's is such a mess. Magazines, coffee cups, dirty laundry. All I want is to lie between clean sheets.

JULIA   Try the morgue?

JANE   Matt always did the laundry.

JULIA   What's the story? Are you over him?

JANE   Yes. No. Yes, I— think— I don't know. I just want to breathe.

JULIA   OK. So what do you think?

JANE   I like it. It's comfortable.

JULIA   You'd have your own room. Some breathing space.

JANE   My apartment's getting crowded.

JULIA   How is Jenna's new boyfriend?

JANE   He moved in.

JULIA   Cozy.

JANE   I think he has a glass eye.

JULIA   He looks funny?

JANE   He doesn't look funny, he just . . . looks funny.

JULIA   Great.

JANE   One night I heard something fall and roll across the floor.

JULIA   His eye?

JANE   Either that or one of her ben-wa balls.

JULIA   Maybe they're interchangeable. So, that should clinch it. What do you say?

JANE   Move in here with you?

JULIA   Why not?

JANE   It sounds like a horrible sitcom. Dumped girl and fired girl live together.

JULIA   We'll hire some guy to clean our rooms in the nude.

JANE   Him or us?

JULIA   New girl chooses. (*Beat.*) All this makes me hungry.

JANE   When in doubt, choose food.

JULIA   How about a burger at Bragg's?

JANE   The ones with the blood oozing out of the fat.

JULIA   You Jane—animal.

(*They get ready to leave.*)

JANE   What about money?

JULIA   I still have some. My treat.

JANE   No, I mean the rent. My share.

JULIA   I can't talk money on an empty stomach. I'll pay more if you take the smaller closet.

JANE   What do you think is harder to understand—love or money?

JULIA   I understand everything I've ever done for love. But I don't understand half the stuff I've done for money.

JANE   I've don't think I've done anything for love. (JANE *is on the brink of tears.*)

JULIA   So—let's start Episode One. Maybe we'll get to season two if it works.

JANE   Just keep breathing.

JULIA   And shake each other if we stop. Keys . . . .

(JULIA *hands* JANE *apartment keys, and they leave the room. Blackout.*)

END OF PLAY

KNOCKOUT

Lisa Bruna

CHARACTERS

Liv: The wife. She is pleasant and attractive, but unfulfilled. 40s–60s.
Morty: The husband. He is dutiful but distracted. 40s–60s.

SETTING

A hotel room.

———————————

(*A mature married couple*, Liv *and* Morty, *are in a hotel room. She flits about, unpacking and settling in to the room as he sits on the edge of the bed pointing the remote at the TV.*)

Morty   I can't find CNN. This happens every time we stay in a hotel.

Liv   I hung the DO NOT DISTURB sign in case you want to get comfy.

Morty   Why can't they stick with the same reliable channel numbers like back in the old days?

Liv   What are you looking for?

Morty   I remember when Channel 4 was NBC, you could stake your life on it. Channel 7 was ABC, Channel 9 was CBS, and UHF was for Jerry Lewis movies.

Liv   What do you want to watch news for anyway? We said we needed this getaway to relax.

Morty   I'm just looking for a headline. I need an update on the crisis overseas so I know how bad my portfolio's getting hit.

Liv   Sweetie, we're on vacation. Relax.

Morty   I can't relax, Liv, because guess what, money never sleeps.

Liv   I'm just afraid you're not going to enjoy this weekend. You look stressed.

(Liv *folds clothing the items she's removed from the suitcase.*)

MORTY   (*Without looking at her.*) And you look gorgeous, baby. As pretty as the day I met you.

LIV   Aw, Morty . . . .

MORTY   I'm serious, honey. I do not care about your forehead wrinkles or the flabby arms, you're still a knockout in my book.

(LIV *pats her fingers against her forehead to feel for wrinkles.*)

LIV   Hey, Morty, do you remember when I had migraines last week, and I stayed in bed watching TV all day? You want to know what I learned that I never knew before?

MORTY   This is ridiculous. Wouldn't you think a national news program would be easier to find? What's this Nickelodeon?

LIV   I found out there's a whole bunch of married couples in this world who want to kill each other.

MORTY   (*Not really paying attention.*) Is that right?

LIV   A hundred percent right. I learned it from this TV show called *Flipped Out*. It's a crime show where the wife literally kills her husband. Or sometimes the husband kills the wife. But usually it's the wife doing the killing, can you believe it?

(LIV *waits, but there is no response from* MORTY.)

Sometimes she plans it out in advance. But sometimes it's like she just *snaps*, you know? One minute she's folding bath towels, the next minute she's mowing down her husband with the family minivan.

MORTY   (*Still distracted.*) Ouch.

(LIV *pulls out two mini bourbons from the mini bar and empties them into two glasses as she speaks.*)

LIV   There's this one woman who killed her husband with antifreeze. Everyone thought he had the flu. But nope! His wife had been spiking his beef stew with antifreeze. Just slooowly poisoning him to death. Here, baby. (*She hands one of the glasses to* MORTY *and* *keeps one for herself as she sidles up next to him on the bed.*) And, by the way, these are true stories, Morty, true stories. They sure do make you wonder about things, like maybe you don't even really know the person lying next to you in the bed.

MORTY   Hmmh. (*He takes a drink.*)

LIV   And the really wacky thing is they had enough shows to run an all-day marathon—back-to-back episodes of these killer couples from morning until almost midnight. So I mean, my god, this kind of thing must just happen all the time, you know? (*She goes back to unpacking as she waits for a response, but* MORTY *stays silent.*) . . . I mean they had enough stories to fill a whole marathon, for gosh sakes.

MORTY   Did you say you know where CNBC is, or no?

(MORTY *extends the remote toward* LIV, *but she doesn't take it.*)

LIV   I thought you said CNN.

MORTY   Or whatever. I just need a damn news reporter to tell me what's going on over there.

LIV   Soooo . . . do you think you could see yourself killing me, Morty? I mean do you think you're the guy who'd just flip out one day and put a pillow over my face? Or would you carefully plot it all out in advance?

MORTY   Plot what out?

LIV   My death, Morty, keep up!

MORTY   What? Why would you ask me something like that?

LIV   Jesus, Morty, are you kidding me? Do you really not know why I'm asking?

MORTY   No, Liv, I genuinely do not know why you are asking me such an outrageous question. Out of the blue!

LIV   Out of the *bl*– . . . okay, maybe if you would listen to me for once in your life . . . .

MORTY   Honey, all I do is listen to you.

LIV   Then you'd know why I'm asking. Think, Morty! What was I just telling you not two minutes ago?

MORTY   I don't know. You said you had a headache. Then I called you a knockout. Then you said something about beef stew. Did we order room service, by the way?

LIV   Okay, beef stew is not the point.

MORTY   Then what *is* the point, Liv?

LIV   The point is I was telling you about a fifteen-hour TV marathon filled with people murdering their spouses! And you don't even care.

MORTY   Oh, yeah, honey, I heard all that.

LIV   And?

MORTY   And what?

LIV   And I want to know . . . can you see yourself *killing* me?

MORTY   Right at this moment . . . ?

LIV   (*Annoyed.*) Okay, never mind.

MORTY   Come on, Liv. Of course not, honey. I'm not even remotely interested in killing you.

LIV   Well, that's a relief.

MORTY   I mean think about it. (*He places his drink on the night stand and gives her slightly more attention than the TV.*) If I were to get locked up, even if my lawyer works out a lesser charge like manslaughter, at my age, I'd never see the light of day again. So, no . . . there's no way I'd risk it. It's just not worth it.

LIV   (*Disappointed.*) I see.

MORTY   And plus, I don't have the instinct for it. Some guys are hard-wired for that sort of thing. Not this guy. And do you know why? I'll tell you why. It's because I have a sharp intellect. I'm frankly just more evolved than most men, so stressful events don't trigger a violent reaction in me. I don't let things bother me that much. Not enough to drive me to murder anyway. That's not who I am. It's not what I want to be known for.

LIV And what do you want to be known for, Morty?

MORTY Let's just say I'm nothing if not an upstanding citizen, you know that, Liv. My mother did not raise a common criminal. If she thought for a second her son was capable of murder, she would kill me with her bare hands.

LIV I see. (*Beat.*) So is that all?

MORTY Yes, Liv, that's all I got. Meanwhile, this TV's got nine hundred-plus channels, and I can't find a goddamned news program.

LIV So you're really going to make this all about you?

MORTY How is this all about *me*? Look, I said I'm not gonna kill you, didn't I? Is that not enough for you?

LIV Well, Morty, if you think that's a satisfactory answer, then who am I to question it? (*She sulks.*)

(MORTY *finally takes a break from the TV to make eye contact with* LIV. *He makes a grand gesture of putting down the remote.*)

MORTY Okay, I give up. What am I supposed to say? What is it you want to hear, Liv, huh?

LIV Oh, I don't know, Morty, just off the top of my head, I might suggest something like "No, darling, I would never kill you . . . *because I love you* . . . and I could never, *ever* kill the woman I *love*?"

MORTY Open your ears, Liv, that's *exactly* what I said.

(MORTY *picks up the remote and turns his attention back to the TV.*)

LIV That's what you said, huh? Really, Morty?

(LIV *walks over to the TV and positions herself next to it in an attempt to gain some of* MORTY'*s attention.*)

MORTY   *Hallll-lllloo.* I just *said* that's what I said, didn't I?

LIV   That's funny because that's not what I heard.

MORTY   Because, as usual, you only hear what you want to hear. (*He angrily points the remote one last time at the TV.*) Dammit, this is unbelievable. I cannot find a news program to save my life!

LIV   Do you even care what *my* answer would be, Morty?

MORTY   (*Helplessly.*) Sure, baby. But first would you mind taking a stab at finding CNN before I lose my mind . . . .

(*As* MORTY *makes the request, he tosses the remote to* LIV. *She tries to block, but it hits her in the head and knocks her out cold. She gives a little squeal as she goes down.* MORTY *rushes to her.*)

Liv! Liv! Baby, talk to me! . . . Liv? Please, Liv!

(*Lights fade to black.*)

END OF PLAY

LOTTO LUCK

Rod McFadden

Original production: Valencia College, Lowndes Shakespeare Center, Orlando, Florida, April 22–23, 2016.

Directed by Bella Celluci.

Cast:

MARGE: Glo Gonzalez

HAL: Christian Bell

Announcer: Bella Celluci

CHARACTERS

MARGE: A suburban wife and mother, 40s, female.
HAL: Her husband, 40s, male.
TV ANNOUNCER: Either gender (*voice-over, or could be visible presence on stage*).

SETTING

A middle class living room.

———————

(*Lights up on Hal and Marge's living room.*)

MARGE   (*Offstage.*) Come on, Hal! Think! Think!

(HAL *crawls in, looking for something that may be on the floor, under a sofa, etc.*)

HAL   It's probably not a winner. It's one in a million.

MARGE   (*Offstage.*) But what if it is? It might be our chance. We gotta find it. Look for it.

 HAL   I am looking! I'm on my hands and knees. How about helping, huh?

(MARGE *enters.*)

MARGE   I'm helping. I'm covering surfaces at eye level. You've got everything else.

HAL   We're not gonna find it. It's gone.

MARGE   It's somewhere! It was right on the kitchen counter.

HAL   It wasn't safe there, so I put it . . . .

MARGE   Yes, Hal? Where did you put it?

HAL   I don't remember. But someplace safer than the kitchen counter.

MARGE   Well, think! The show's already started.

(MARGE *clicks the TV remote.*)

TV Announcer   (*Voice-over.*) . . . and the super mega bonus ball number is seven!

Marge   We always play seven for the bonus ball!

(Hal *quickens his search.*)

TV Announcer   Our state-of-the-art Lotto Tracker has verified that one ticket, sold in Brentwood, has matched all six numbers, plus the super mega bonus ball! So, yes, we do have a potential winner in this one and only . . . billion-dollar drawing.

Marge   Hear that, Hal? Brentwood. Where you bought our ticket, right?

Hal   Yeah. I stopped for gas on my way home.

TV Announcer   The gas station owner who sold the ticket collects a cool million, but the person who bought it might be the winner of the biggest jackpot in history.

Marge   Gas station! It must be us. Don't just stand there. Find it.

(*Their search intensifies, until the* Announcer*'s voice transfixes them again on the set.*)

TV Announcer   The winning numbers again are: Four, twelve, twenty-one, twenty-eight, thirty-seven, and forty-four. With the super mega bonus number, seven.

Marge   Hal, are those the numbers you played?

Hal   I know I picked seven for the bonus, but I just took random numbers for the rest. I . . . I don't remember what they were.

Marge   You can't remember where you put the ticket, either!

TV Announcer   The ticket holder must call us in the next sixty seconds, or they forfeit this once-in-a-lifetime, billion-dollar prize. Vanna, start the countdown! Call in now and read off the unique security code printed on the back of the winning ticket. But hurry. Only fifty-two seconds left!!

Marge   Great! Just great! You've lost our winning ticket!

HAL It's not a winning ticket! How do you don't know it's the winning ticket?

MARGE Because you lost it! Every week, for twenty-two years you've never lost our ticket. And it's never been a winner!

HAL That's your proof? Because it's never been the winner before.

MARGE And because you lost it!!

TV ANNOUNCER Only thirty seconds remain. If you have that ticket, stop jumping for joy and call in now.

(MARGE *grabs* HAL *by his collar and shakes him.*)

MARGE Where did you put that ticket? Think, Hal. Think, you idiot!

TV ANNOUNCER Twenty-three seconds left to call.

HAL Honey, forget it. Like you said, we never win! I'm ninety-nine percent sure those aren't the numbers I picked.

MARGE That still leaves a one-percent chance! You know what one percent of a billion is? Ten million! It's like a hundred percent chance at ten million bucks! Think what it could mean! A bigger house, in a nice neighborhood. A better car. We could send Kathy to a good college. We could have whatever we wanted. We could be . . . happy again. You heard him. Brentwood, gas station, mega bonus number seven. We've gotta find that ticket!

HAL Okay. Okay.

TV ANNOUNCER It's the final ten seconds. You must call now. There is no second chance. Ten.

MARGE Come on! Where did you put it?

TV ANNOUNCER Nine. Eight.

HAL I don't know. I wanted to put it where I'd never lose it.

TV ANNOUNCER Seven. Six.

MARGE Maybe it's still in the kitchen. Maybe it fell behind the fridge.

TV Announcer   Five. Four.

(Marge *rushes off.* Hal *stops and thinks.*)

TV Announcer   Three. Two. One. (B*eat.*) Oh, I'm sorry. Time is up. Well, America, I guess we'll never know who held that winning ticket. But somewhere, tomorrow morning, some dumb schmuck is gonna to see those numbers on the news. And when he takes that ticket from his wallet . . .

(Hal *has a revelation. He takes his wallet from his back pocket.*)

. . . at least he'll know . . .

(Hal *removes a lotto ticket from the wallet, and looks at it.* Marge*'s voice startles him.*)

Marge   (*Offstage, approaching.*) No, it's not here either.

(Marge *enters.* Hal *puts his wallet away and crumples the ticket, hiding it behind his back.*)

TV Announcer   . . . He'll know for the rest of his long, unhappy life that he could've won a billion dollars.

(Marge *turns off the TV. Behind her back,* Hal *eats the ticket.* Marge *turns back to him.*)

Marge   Well, it really was a long shot, wasn't it? But it felt nice to dream again, if only for a little while.

(Hal *nods as he tries to swallow the ticket.*)

I suppose we'll never know.

(Hal *shakes his head.*)

Unless the ticket turns up.

(Hal *shrugs and nods.* Marge *goes to* Hal.)

Do you think we'll ever find it?

(Hal *swallows one final hard gulp.*)

Hal   Uh, no, dear.

(*Lights fade down.*)

End of Play

MARY'S EDDIE

A PLAY BY Y YORK, INSPIRED BY THE TALENTS OF MARY LOUISE BURKE

Y York

Mary's Eddie was presented by the Northwest Playwrights Alliance at Seattle Repertory Theatre, December 2009, directed by Cynthia White. Subsequently presented by Play with Your Lunch in March 2011, directed by Herb Duval.

CHARACTERS

MARY AND EDDIE: They are in their 60s.

TIME

The present.

SETTING

A living room.

(*A living room.* MARY *is alone with her cocktail.* EDDIE *enters. He wears half glasses. He half enters.*)

EDDIE   Do you know where the checkbook is?

MARY   I think it's still in my bag.

EDDIE   Which is where?

MARY   On the counter.

EDDIE   You should put it back when you're done with it.

(EDDIE *starts to leave.*)

MARY   I'm never done with it.

EDDIE   (*Half returns.*) You're not using it now.

MARY   But I'll have to go out again, won't I? I'll have to go out for beer or potato chips or charcoal. Checkbook items.

EDDIE   If you put it back, I wouldn't have to bother you.

MARY   You're not bothering me, Eddie. I like these little intimate moments we have—"Where's the checkbook? Have you seen my car keys? Bring me a roll of toilet paper."

(*He stares at her a moment.*)

MARY   Where does it go? The checkbook.

EDDIE   You know where it goes because that's where you find it because that's where I put it when I'm done with it.

MARY What are you going to buy?

EDDIE Nothing.

MARY Then why do you need the checkbook?

EDDIE QuickBooks.

MARY Can't it wait? Aren't you sick of that? Aren't you sick of looking at numbers all day long?

EDDIE I don't like it to mount up.

MARY It's in my bag. (*He exits.*)

(*A longish pause.* MARY *glances about, including at the empty seat next to her. Then* MARY *has a conversation.*)

MARY *Is that seat taken, Miss?*

No, but I'm waiting for someone.

Is he late?

. . . As a matter of fact he is a little late.

I can't imagine being late to meet someone as sweet and lovely as you.

What?

I said—

I heard what you said, I just can't believe it.

EDDIE (*Off.*) Mary?

(EDDIE *enters.*)

MARY What? I didn't say anything.

EDDIE (*He holds up a jaunty purse.*) Is this new?

MARY Yes. Do you like it?

EDDIE I have no idea if I like it.

MARY I hoped you'd like it. It's "saucy." (*Takes it.*) I can sling it over my shoulder and it just hits my hip when I walk, drawing attention to my sexy walk—that's what the salesgirl said. It makes me look saucy. Do you think I look saucy?

EDDIE   . . . How much did it cost?

MARY   It's a knockoff.

EDDIE   What does that mean?

MARY   That means thirty-five dollars.

EDDIE   That much?

MARY   Thirty-five as opposed to three hundred and ninety.

(EDDIE *exits shaking his head. Brief pause, then* MARY *continues.*)

MARY   *Did you know that man, Miss?*

Not at all. He must have mistaken us for other people.

Does that happen often here?

Yes, it does, almost every day.

Maybe we should leave.

Oh. Oh, no. I can't leave.

Then, may I sit down until your friend comes?

Oh, no.

But what if that deranged man returns?

Oh.

I'll leave as soon as someone comes who can protect you.

(*She looks toward the other room. Brief pause.*)

I'm not usually this forward, Miss. It's your eyes. That's what made me come over in this bold fashion. I am not a bold man. But your eyes, and how they sit in your face, there's this softness, this cushion in your eyes that says a person might place something fragile in them, a fragile something, a piece of fragile knowledge, and all your softness might envelop it so that it doesn't break.

(*Slight pause.*)

Do you mean I'm fat?

Oh, no, no. You're beautiful. Why would you say you're fat?

No, I—I just didn't know what you meant about my cushion.

I meant you look like you can be trusted. With precious knowledge.

(EDDIE *enters, looking fiercely at the checkbook.*)

Oh, no, I never tell a secret, but I don't like them. I hate the burden they place on my heart.

(EDDIE *looks around to see who she is talking to.*)

It's not a secret, I didn't mean a secret. Secrets do hurt. I meant, your eyes. You seem like a person who might let another person be himself. Your eyes are so relaxed and kind.

Are you an optometrist?

No. I'm an accountant.

(EDDIE's *jaw drops. He looks briefly at the checkbook in his hand.*)

You seem sort of romantic for an accountant.

Would you . . . would you like to dance?

I would. I would really like that. No one ever asks me.

(MARY *dances.* EDDIE *looks on, softly.*)

When I was a girl in school, the nuns told us that boys would try to feel us up if we danced with them so we should only dance with boys who we planned to marry.

When I was young, if a girl let me dance with her, I felt like I was holding her soul. I must tread so carefully. She was precious and I must have great care. One hand is allowed to touch yours, so firm and dry, while my other hand holds you so that we might move together as one. I know so much about you already. Your eyes, how light you are on your feet, the feel of your waist against my hand. It's a forever moment. I would like to kiss you.

Oh! No. You can't kiss me. I don't even know your name.

EDDIE   Eddie! (*A pause.* MARY *freezes.*) . . . My name is Eddie.

(MARY *looks in front of her.* EDDIE *looks at* MARY.)

END OF PLAY

MODERN ART MODELING

Rod McFadden

Original production took place at Valencia College, Lowndes Shakespeare Center, Orlando, Florida, on April 23, 2016. It was directed by Isabel Hernandez with the following cast:

BRITNEY: Sarah Hart
ARTIST: Gabriel Resto

CHARACTERS

BRITNEY: A cheerleader and aspiring actress, 20s, female.
ARTIST: 20s, male.

SETTING

An artist's studio.

(*Lights up on an artist's studio.* BRITNEY *is wearing only a bathrobe. Across the stage,* ARTIST *paints a canvas on an easel, which faces away from the audience.*)

ARTIST   Yes, you can put your clothes back on now.

BRITNEY   So you got, um . . . all of me, huh?

ARTIST   I'm not quite done. But you can get dressed now. Just a few last details to finish it.

(BRITNEY *goes behind a folding screen to dress.*)

BRITNEY   (*From behind the screen.*) I can't wait to see. What's it called again?

ARTIST   *Naked Woman.*

BRITNEY   I really appreciate you letting me do this modeling thing, 'cuz I think it's a good step for my actress resume, you know. Even if it is naked modeling. Now, don't get me wrong, 'cuz I don't have any problem with, like . . . open nuditivity, or people wanting to celebrate their physical form. Though some people's forms are not exactly cause for celebration, if you know what I mean.

Even so, it's all okay with me. Whatever sets your ringtone, right? But as a member of the Clara Vista pep squad, I'm held to a higher standard of morality than your average student. So I couldn't tell anyone about what I've been doing here.

ARTIST   Please, some quiet. These last touches are critical.

BRITNEY   Oh, right. I know how it is when you're being all artistic, and people don't get what you're trying to do. It's like when I'm doing a cheer. People think it's just a lot of jumping and yelling, but there's some real choreographical aspects to it that people just don't appreciate.

ARTIST   Yes, and it's the same for me right now. So please. Quiet.

(BRITNEY, *now dressed, tiptoes out from behind the screen, holding a finger to her lips, to stop any noise.* ARTIST *makes a few deft strokes of the brush, then steps back and admires his work.*)

BRITNEY   Is it . . . done?

ARTIST   Yes. *Naked Woman* is finished. And you've been part of something historic. This piece will revolutionize modern portraiture.

BRITNEY   It's pretty exciting. Though I feel a little weird, about me hanging there in the Colfax Art Museum. All naked and all.

ARTIST   This piece will never hang in the Colfax. I have not created it to be displayed in some pedestrian little gallery on a second-rate community college campus. *Naked Woman* shall hang in the Pompidou Center, or the Tate, or New York's MoMA.

BRITNEY   Oh. Well, that's better anyway. No one in the pep squad's gonna see it if it's way out in New York somewhere. But I get to take a picture of it for my portfolio thingy, right? I mean, that was the deal.

ARTIST   Yes, of course.

BRITNEY   So, can I see it? How do I look?

ARTIST   Yours may be the first eyes to gaze upon my *Naked Woman*.

BRITNEY   Well, it's nothing I haven't seen already, right?
(*She gets her iPhone ready to take a picture.*)
It'll be like a selfie of a selfie. Though I don't do naked selfies. I have a rule about that.

(*She comes around the easel to see the picture.*)

ARTIST Behold . . . Naked Woman.

BRITNEY Hey! What the hey?

(BRITNEY *takes the canvas from the easel and* ARTIST *quickly takes it from her.*)

ARTIST Careful. Careful. It is a modern masterwork.

BRITNEY I'm not even there. It's just an outline of me. You painted all around it. You didn't paint me at all.

ARTIST Yes, the negative space subverts the viewer's expectations. It forces him to see something in himself that he's trying to hide.

BRITNEY Yeah, okay. But where am I? I'm not even in it.

ARTIST Exactly. Disappointing him. Frustrating his voyeuristic urges. It forces the viewer to confront his repressed need to treat naked women as objects of his rampant sexual desire.

BRITNEY But there's just a blank space where I'm supposed to be.

ARTIST Yes. That's the whole point.

BRITNEY Well, it's a stupid point. If you weren't gonna put me in the picture, why'd I have to sit here with no clothes on every night for the last two weeks?

ARTIST My artistic integrity demanded it. Anyone can paint around a section of blank canvas. To create *Naked Woman*, I needed to actively omit a real naked woman from the work. So your presence here—

BRITNEY My naked presence.

ARTIST Yes, your actual presence here, but not on the canvas, fills the piece with Truth. It elevates *Naked Woman* to the level of Masterwork.

BRITNEY Well, lah-dee-dah. What about my portfolio? How will anyone know it's me?

ARTIST   That's not important. Only the Art matters.

BRITNEY   You know what I think? I think you're one of those perverts.

ARTIST   I am an artist.

BRITNEY   Yeah. A perverted artist.
>   (BRITNEY *turns to leave, then stops.*)
>   And I have just one more thing to say to you.
>   (*Half spoken, half cheered.*)
>   Ready, okay.
>   You think you made a masterwork
>   But you are just a stupid jerk.

(BRITNEY *exits.* ARTIST *returns to the easel and admires his work.*)

END OF PLAY

MOON JUICE

Grace Trotta

Moon Juice was originally produced by Valencia College Theater in collaboration with Playwrights Round Table at the Orlando Shakespeare Theater on April 22nd, 2016. The original cast was as follows: Rose Cambron as Tina, Jean Campos as Taylor, and Yomira Pou McDonald as Elise.

CHARACTERS

TINA: A woman in her late 20s or early 30s. TAYLOR's sister.
TAYLOR: A man in his early 20s. In an anesthesia-induced daze for
the duration of the scene.
ELISE: A woman in her 20s or 30s.

TIME

The present.

SETTING

A coffee shop. Two chairs, set up at one table.

(*At rise:* ELISE *is seated in one of the chairs.* TAYLOR *and* TINA *stand off to
one side.*)

TINA   Okay, Taylor. I am going to get you a smoothie. Just find a
seat and I'll bring it to you. I'll be right back. Nod your head so I
know that you understand.

(TAYLOR *nods.*)

Good. I'll be back.

(TINA *exits.* TAYLOR *spits a wad of cotton gauze into his palm, puts it in
his pocket, then scans the room lazily, dropping into the other chair.*)

ELISE   Hi, are you Taylor?

TAYLOR   That's my name, don't wear it out.

ELISE   Nice to meet you, I'm Elise. Your friend, John, gave me
your number?

TAYLOR   Okeydokey. He's a good guy I guess. I love him.

ELISE   So you guys are pretty close?

(TAYLOR *stares into space, intensely.*)

Sorry, this is awkward. I don't really know how these things work.
I guess I'll just jump right in, then. So, uh, what do you do?

TAYLOR   Oh, pretty much I just ball hard. All day, every day. I'm a baller.

(TAYLOR *is tearing a napkin into tiny pieces.*)

ELISE   You mean you're a basketball player or what?

TAYLOR   (*He sighs deeply.*) One time in summer camp I got hit really hard with a basketball when I was trying to catch it. I broke my finger. Then I had to go home for the rest of the summer.

ELISE   I mean, what do you do for work? Like, I'm an administrative assistant. And you are . . . ?

TAYLOR   That sounds pretty fancy. You're way fancier than me. I went to a fancy restaurant one time and they had the soft lap blankets.

ELISE   Napkins?

TAYLOR   Now you're speaking my language, buddy.
    (TAYLOR *points the "finger guns" gesture at* ELISE. *He imitates a laser gun.*)
    Pew, pew, pew. Nailed it.

ELISE   (*Laughing weakly.*) Okay. I guess we can change the subject.
    (TAYLOR *arranges the napkin scraps into piles.*)
    What kind of music are you into?

TAYLOR   The funky kind, mostly. I don't know. Music is like, the thing of where it sounds like colors, right?

ELISE   I guess. That an interesting way to put it. You know, music. Like bands and stuff? I really like the Beatles.

TAYLOR   (*In a bad British accent.*) Here they are, The Beatles!

ELISE   Exactly, yeah. Are you a fan?

TAYLOR   Why? Are you warm?

(*An uncomfortable silence.*)

ELISE   Did you want to order some coffee?

(TAYLOR *looks around in a panic, remembering* TINA.)

TAYLOR   Oh no. Oh my goodness, oh dear.

ELISE   Is anything wrong?

(TAYLOR *puts his head down on the table.*)

TAYLOR   I lost my sister. She's gone forever.

ELISE   Oh my God, I'm so sorry. Did you want to talk about it? Taylor? It's going to be okay. Please don't cry.

(TAYLOR *lifts his head in defiance.*)

TAYLOR   I am NOT crying, Miss Missy! I got some moon juice. Methinks I am allergic to it.

ELISE   Is that like an *X-Files* thing? Where did you get the moon juice?

TAYLOR   The mouth doctor put it in my arm. So he could take my teeth back to his lair.

(TINA *returns, carrying two drinks.*)

ELISE   Oh. That's nice.

TINA   (*To* TAYLOR.)

There you are! What are you doing?

(*To* ELISE.)

I'm sorry about that. My brother just had his wisdom teeth out and he doesn't know which way is up right now. I hope he didn't bother you too much. Taylor, let's go.

ELISE   That makes a lot of sense. I was kind of set up on a blind date sort of thing, so I just assumed this was it.

TINA   I guess you were pretty disappointed when this doofus showed up instead, huh?

ELISE   Right. I mean, Taylor is typically a girl's name, so there's that too.

TAYLOR   Hold on just a darn second!
(*Pointing to* ELISE.)
So if you're gay . . .
(*Pointing to* TINA.)
and you're gay, then who's driving the bus?

TINA   (*Embarrassed.*) Okay, pal! Time to go home!

ELISE   (*Reaching into purse.*) Wait a second.
(ELISE *hands a business card to* ELISE.)
This is kind of forward, but here. Give me a call when you're done babysitting. If you want.

TINA   Sounds good. Nice meeting you.
(TINA *guides* TAYLOR *offstage. To* TAYLOR, *quietly:*)
Thanks, doofus.

TAYLOR   (*Taking a sip of his smoothie.*) And thank you, moon juice.

END OF PLAY

OUT TO LUNCH

Judy Klass

Out to Lunch has a long history as a comedy sketch. As a short play, in its present form, it was first produced by working theatre collective in February 2011. Eva Suter was the director, and Samantha Luhn played Margaret, Meredith Ott played Sue, and Renew Gerow played Alan.

CHARACTERS

ALAN: Tries to see himself as an office charmer—quite thrown when women are not charmed. 20–60.

MARGARET: Indignant at the behavior of guys like ALAN; she has been waiting, perhaps, for such a confrontation. 20–50.

SUE: A bit more meek and tentative than the other two. 20–50.

TIME

The present.

SETTING

In an alternate universe.

———————

(*At rise: In a business office,* MARGARET *sits working at her desk.* ALAN *approaches, slightly nervous, trying to be casual.*)

ALAN Well, Margaret, how's it going? Have you gotten through all the files yet?

MARGARET Most of them. But there were a few things that needed to be handled immediately. I left a thumb drive on your desk.

ALAN Oh, sure, I'll take care of them. Wow, you seem so energized! Where did you sleep last night?

MARGARET With Gary, in marketing. Why?

ALAN Oh, no reason. Um, Margaret?

MARGARET Yes?

ALAN Well, are you busy at the moment?

MARGARET No. No, I was thinking of taking a break, actually.

ALAN Great. Um, I was wondering, would you like to have sex with me?

MARGARET What? You mean, right now?

Alan   Well, yeah, now. You weren't planning on having it with anyone else, were you?

Margaret   Well, no . . . .

Alan   And most everyone has left already. No sense in each of us going off to have it alone. Why are you looking at me so suspiciously?

Margaret   Alan. You want to have sex with me . . . and then what?

Alan   What do you mean?

Margaret   Just what exactly is this leading up to?

Alan   It's not leading up to anything. I just want to have a little light, friendly sex with a friend.

Margaret   Look Alan, don't play games with me, all right? I'm not stupid.

(*Pause.*)

You want to have lunch with me. Don't you.

Alan   (*Shocked.*) Lunch! Hold on, I never even suggested . . . .

Margaret   Sure, you invite a girl out for sex, and you expect it to just smoothly segue into some hot, steamy little meal for two.

Alan   God, you're paranoid. I think you know me better than that.

Margaret   Mmm. And where do you propose we have this so-called "sex?"

Alan   Well, I don't know, I thought we could go back to my apartment.

Margaret   Oh, right, I see, back at your apartment. Where you've got your fridge and freezer, your microwave, your Cuisinart, your waffle iron . . . .

Alan   How do you know I have all that?

Margaret   (*Indignant.*) How? Because I've heard you bragging. Every woman in this office has heard you bragging to the guys about the salads you toss. About how you take a girl home for sex, and soon you've, you've got her at the table, licking out the bowls and snuffling up the crumbs . . . .

ALAN (*With bravado.*) All right, that's it, I've had it. You know, I try to get a rapport going with my female colleagues. I make an effort. But you cynical modern women—you see a guy being friendly, and your mind jumps from sex to lunch in an instant. Well, never again.

(HE *storms off.* SHE *calls after him, angrily.*)

MARGARET Not with me, anyway!

(SUE *enters, carrying a brown bag.* SHE *tries to sneak by.*)

Hello, Sue.

(SUE *jumps nervously.* MARGARET *is still caught up in her own troubles.*)

SUE Oh! Hi, Margaret, how's it going?

MARGARET Not so good.

SUE Why, what's wrong?

MARGARET Alan the galloping gourmet strikes again.

SUE Oh no.

MARGARET I know I shouldn't let him get to me. But, God, when he's standing over you, practically licking his chops . . . .

(SUE, *agitated, is again trying to sneak by, hiding the bag behind her back.* MARGARET *sniffs the air, and tries to get a peek at it.*)

MARGARET Sue . . . where are you going? And what are you carrying in that suspicious-looking brown paper bag?

SUE (*Guiltily.*) A roast beef sandwich.

MARGARET (*Scandalized, grinning.*) What! On the premises?

SUE Ssshhh!

MARGARET Oops. Sorry.

(SUE *decides to spill her heart.*)

Sue   I finally agreed to share one with Bill. I spread on pickles, and mustard . . . and he—he never even showed up.

(*Crying.*)

I feel so ashamed.

Margaret   (*Moved.*) You poor kid. That's awful. I swear, the guys around here can be such freaking jerks.

Sue   I was so excited, thinking about it all day. And now, who will I share it with?

(Margaret *considers for a moment.*)

Margaret   Um, Sue . . . that mustard. Is it Grey Poupon?

(Sue *nods.* Margaret *looks around furtively.*)

Sue . . . would you like it if, maybe . . . I shared that sandwich with you?

(She *whips off her glasses, and looks at* Sue *directly.*)

Sue   (*Stunned.*) Do we dare?

Margaret   Let's go. My car's out front.

(*They exit, running and giggling.*)

End of Play

OVERSTUFFED

A COUCH PLAY

Lee Blessing

Overstuffed was originally produced at the Playwrights' Center, Minneapolis, Minnesota, in the fall of 2011.

CHARACTERS

SOFIE DAVENPORT: 18, a total mess.
DIANE DAVENPORT: 40s, totally put together.

TIME

The present.

SETTING

The Davenport home.

————————

(*Lights up. An old, well-worn, overstuffed couch. A moment goes by. One of the cushions on the couch starts to move slightly. A finger emerges beneath it, then another, then a hand. An entire arm works its way out of the couch from beneath the cushions. Once its struggle is over, the arm drapes down, hand on the floor. Another moment passes. A low chanting emanates from under the cushions. The words can't be discerned at first. They become clearer as more of the person in the couch—*SOFIE DAVENPORT—*is seen. She wears dirty sweatpants and a T-shirt. She's eighteen, and at her worst.*)

SOFIE   (*Chanting.*) Eating oreos masturbating drinking sleeping watching TV smoking dope eating mini oreos tweeting drunken rock stars watching TV news eating double stuf oreos sleeping masturbating smoking dope reading porn eating chocolate crème oreos masturbating drinking tweeting reality stars eating banana split crème oreos tweeting celebrity felons sleeping watching porn eating double delight oreos cool mint crème oreos golden oreos fudge covered oreos oreo cakesters oreo fudgees strawberry milkshake crème oreos . . . masturbating masturbating masturbating masturbating calling Mom Hey Mom

(SOFIE's *mother,* DIANE, *enters. She's bright, cheery, in her mid-forties. Unlike her daughter, she's completely put together and at her most attractive.*)

DIANE   Hi, Honey. Is something wrong?

SOFIE   Do we have any Oreos?

DIANE   We certainly do. We have every variety, including inside-out ones. *But*, if you wait for me to get back from the store, I'll bring the new Halloween ones with the orange filling.

SOFIE   Okay . . . .

DIANE   Great. And while you're waiting I'll bring in a few bags of just plain Oreos.

SOFIE   I can get 'em—

DIANE   No, no. You'll burn calories. Save your energy for homework. Where's your computer?

SOFIE   It's, um . . . .
(*Pulling a laptop out from under a cushion.*)
Here.

DIANE   Flip it open, turn off the porn sites, and learn something. You have a test tomorrow, don't you?

SOFIE   Yeah . . . .

DIANE   And you're going to ace it, aren't you? Like you always do?

SOFIE   Yeah . . . .

DIANE   You make me so proud. Never get a single answer wrong. You're going to be a legend in the annals of online education.

SOFIE   I don't know . . . .

DIANE   I do. I am so happy I home-schooled you. This is a wonderful time, Sofie Davenport. All our dreams are coming true.
(*Turning for the kitchen, then turning back.*)
Oh, Sofie. I was in the bathroom a minute ago, and I noticed a lot of throw up.

SOFIE   I'm sorry. I'll clean it up.

DIANE   No, no. Stay there. I'm happy to do it, and I'm really not mad about the mess. It's just that . . . .

SOFIE   What?

DIANE   Well . . . bulimia really isn't our goal, is it? I mean, what's the point of eating all those cookies if you're not going to keep them down, right? They don't do you any good at all that way.

SOFIE   I suppose. It's just . . . a lot, you know . . . of cookies.

DIANE   And thank God, too. Thank God they make that many cookies! Thank God there will always be enough cookies for girls like you and the parents who love them. Because right now, dear, you still do not weigh nearly enough.

SOFIE   I know.

DIANE   Don't be discouraged. You're doing really well in school, and on the appearance side of things, you're way ahead.

SOFIE   Really? You think so?

DIANE   Yes, I do. And it's not easy for you, either. Because you are naturally very attractive.

SOFIE   I'm sorry.

DIANE   It's not your fault. But I know right now that's a terrible cross to bear. But if you stay with the program, I promise, people will completely forget how good you used to look. Before you know it, my darling—and I mean this from the bottom of my heart—you *will* achieve the Three "S"s. Smart. Slovenly. Stuffed.

SOFIE   You really think so?

DIANE   Yes. Only we're going to have to get you a lot more stuffed. A lot more. Much, much, much, much more. Because while there are men who love smart girls, and men who love really, really big girls and even men who like girls who are a total mess—which reminds me. Arm.

   (SOFIE *raises an arm over her head.* DIANE *smells her daughter's armpit and reels at the odor.*)
   Whew! Good! How long since you washed?

SOFIE   A week?

DIANE   Excellent! The point is, no man can get passionate about a woman who's smart, huge *and* smells like a garbage can.

SOFIE   Are you sure?

DIANE   Absolutely. I know what I had to do to get your father out of *my* life. It is so much harder when the man is already there and obsessed. They don't let go.

SOFIE   No.

DIANE   They never let go. They get obsessed with you.

SOFIE   Yeah . . . .

DIANE   And then they try to kill you. What is the leading cause of death for women between eighteen and thirty-five?

SOFIE   Men.

DIANE   Men. Men. Seven court orders didn't stop him. Seven. Each time he showed up and hurt me worse. The last two times, he nearly killed me. And why? Because it took me so long to get fat enough. Well, you remember.

(*As* SOFIE *nods.*)

But I transformed myself, didn't I? My darling girl?

SOFIE   Yes.

DIANE   I made myself smarter, fatter, stinkier—that was my mantra. I had to get up to 376 pounds—it was barely enough. And I had to smell like . . . Fresh Kills—you remember that dump? You don't have to; you remember me.

(SOFIE *nods again.*)

And he finally lost interest. Because I persevered. I knew the law wouldn't help me. I knew I'd be dead and you'd be alone. I helped myself, just like you're doing. And you get a head start, isn't that wonderful? There's no man in your life. Only this couch and food and TV and porn and masturbation and your university, right here in this box. I wish I'd been as lucky when I was your age.

SOFIE   I really do feel lucky.

DIANE   And there's such a beautiful light at the end of the tunnel, honey. A whole rainbow. Once you're in your forties and men *finally* don't give a shit about you anyway? You can lose all that weight and clean up and walk out the front door, into a world of human beings who do not look at how cute you are and become homicidal.

SOFIE   That sounds great.

DIANE   Doesn't it? Look at me now. I cleaned up pretty good, didn't I?

SOFIE   Yeah.

DIANE   And you will, too. In time.

SOFIE   You're beautiful, Mom.

DIANE   So are you, Sofie. So are you.

(*They smile and embrace.* DIANE *reels a bit when she gets a sudden whiff of her daughter, then shares a smile with her and settles into the embrace once more. Lights fade to black.*)

END OF PLAY

PILLOW TALK

Eric Grant

CHARACTERS

PATRICIA: 30s, delightfully dotty.
FRANCIS: 50s, serious, tired.

TIME

Afternoon.

SETTING

A bedroom. Maybe it's a hotel, maybe it's a house. It is unclear.

———————————

(PATRICIA *is lying in bed, her head hanging off the side.* FRANCIS *is at his desk, writing something.*)

PATRICIA   I think it sounds classier.

FRANCIS   Hmm?

PATRICIA   "Having an affair." It sounds more dignified than "cheating on you."

(FRANCIS *stops writing for a moment.*)

FRANCIS   Are you cheating on me?

PATRICIA   No, darling, just thinking out loud.

FRANCIS   Ah.

PATRICIA   What if I were?

FRANCIS   Hmm?

PATRICIA   Having an affair. Would you be upset?

FRANCIS   I . . . suppose I don't know.

PATRICIA   What about Tommy? What if he was . . . ?

FRANCIS   We agreed not to talk about them.

PATRICIA   I'm sorry.

FRANCIS   Besides his name isn't Tommy.

PATRICIA   It's not?

FRANCIS   No.

PATRICIA   What is it then?

FRANCIS   I'm not telling you.

PATRICIA   Don't make me guess.

FRANCIS   The less you know, the better.

(*Pause.*)

PATRICIA   It's drafty in here.

FRANCIS   Oh, I opened the window in the bathroom, maybe that's why.

PATRICIA   Hmm . . . (*Pause.*) What are you writing?

FRANCIS   My suicide note.

PATRICIA   No, really.

   (*No response.*)

   Is it a chapter of your memoir?

FRANCIS   Hmm.

PATRICIA   I can't wait to read it.

FRANCIS   You won't.

PATRICIA   Why not?!

FRANCIS   It'll be published after my death.

PATRICIA   Like you're so important.

FRANCIS   With a clause that bans family from reading it.

PATRICIA   I'm hardly family . . . .

FRANCIS   You're listed in the will as part of the group of people not allowed—

PATRICIA   I'm mentioned in your will?

FRANCIS   Hmm? Oh. Yes. Didn't I tell you?

PATRICIA   (*Sitting up and grinning.*) No . . . .

FRANCIS   Well . . . You are. (*Beat.*) Why did you say that?

PATRICIA   What?

FRANCIS   That I'm not important.

PATRICIA   I didn't say you weren't important . . . I just meant . . . Well, sure you're important! I was just . . . I was just being a big jerk, is that what you want me to say? I'm sorry.

FRANCIS   It's all right, don't go to pieces over it.

PATRICIA   I'm not going to pieces over it! (*Pause.*) Is Meyer going to make you deputy governor?

FRANCIS   Hmm.

PATRICIA   That's nice. (*Pause.*) Do you not want the job?
(FRANCIS *stops writing. He looks off.*)
Francis . . . ?
(*She looks at him for a beat before going back to look at the ceiling. After a moment, she sits up with a revelation.*)
It's Tony, isn't it!

FRANCIS   Hmm?

PATRICIA   Your husband's name! It's Tony.

(*Lights out.*)

END OF PLAY

PRESS PRAY

Seth Freeman

CHARACTERS

MARTIN: A desperate soul.
VOICE FROM ABOVE: Response.

TIME

Off-hours.

SETTING

In the dark, sirens, traffic. Lights up on a house of worship, the setting only suggested: a couple of pews, a cross perhaps or other symbol, multicolored light splashed in the from the side and above, as from stained-glass windows.

———————

(MARTIN *enters, ducks behind a pew. Blue/red lights wash the set. Police or emergency vehicles seem to pass by.* MARTIN *enters further. Whatever his exact age, appearance, background, and other circumstances, all that matters now is that he is desperate and anxious, a man in some sort of trouble. He clasps his hands together, kneels or sits, composes himself for prayer.*)

MARTIN   Oh, God.

VOICE FROM ABOVE   Please listen carefully as this menu has changed.

> (MARTIN *jumps, startled. He looks around resumes a prayerful posture.*)
>
> For English press or say "one." Para español oprima o diga el "dos." For all other languages press or say "three."
>
> (MARTIN *swallows hard, again looks around uncertainly.*)
>
> For English press or say "one." Para español oprima o diga el "dos." For all other languages—

MARTIN   (*Uncertainly.*) One.

VOICE FROM ABOVE   —press or say "three."

MARTIN   One. *One!*

VOICE FROM ABOVE   Thank you for your interest in our service. If this is a true spiritual emergency, please stop this prayer and dial the number on the inside cover of your hymnal.

(MARTIN *tentatively lifts the hymnal in the compartment of the pew before him.*)

Otherwise, please wait and your prayers will be answered in the order in which they were received.We are experiencing unusually prayer high volume, so we apologize for any delays. At the end of your prayer you will be asked to respond to a brief questionnaire. All right, let's get started. For prayers of Repentance press or say "two." For prayers of Supplication press or say "three." For prayers of Redemption press or say "four." For prayers of Forgiveness press or say "five." For all other prayers press or say "six."

MARTIN   I guess . . . Er . . . Supplic—three. Three.

VOICE FROM ABOVE   I think you said, "Two." Is this correct?

MARTIN   No.

VOICE FROM ABOVE   Okay, let's try that again. For prayers of Repentance press or say "two." For prayers of

Supplication press or say "three." For—

MARTIN   Three.

VOICE FROM ABOVE   Prayers of—

MARTIN   (*Frustrated.*) Three!

VOICE FROM ABOVE   —say "four." For prayers of Forgiveness press or say "five." For all other prayers press or say "six."

MARTIN   Three.

VOICE FROM ABOVE   I think you said, "Three." Is this correct?

MARTIN   Yes. Correct. Three. Yes.

VOICE FROM ABOVE   You requested prayers of Supplication. Please say the category for which you are supplicating. If you are praying for help with a personal problem, say "Problem." If you are praying for a material object like a new Lexus, say "Car."

MARTIN   Uh . . . .

VOICE FROM ABOVE   I'm sorry. I did not understand your answer. Please repeat your answer slowly and clearly.

MARTIN   I'm in trouble. Nothing . . . makes sense . . . .

VOICE FROM ABOVE   I think you said, Vengeance. Is this correct?

MARTIN   No.

PHONE VOICE   Good, because Vengeance is mine. Please repeat your answer slowly and clearly.

MARTIN   Prob. Lem.

VOICE FROM ABOVE   I think you said, "Problem." Is this correct?

MARTIN   Yes. Correct.

VOICE FROM ABOVE   Let me connect you to that department.

(*Hold music:* Pachelbel, Canon in D—*but a cheery, treacly, hold music version.*)

Please wait. Your prayer is important to us. It will be answered in the order received.

(*Hold music.* MARTIN *taps his fingers.*)

We appreciate your patience and look forward to being of service.

(*Hold music.* MARTIN *stands up, sits.*)

Thank you for your patience. We apologize for the inconvenience. Please state the problem with which you would like help. For example, if you would like the Lord to help heal someone who is sick, you could say, "Illness." If you would like the Lord to aid you in making a woman who barely knows you exist interested in you romantically, you could say, "Wingman," or simply, "Hard up."

MARTIN   Okay, enough. I give up.

VOICE FROM ABOVE   I'm sorry. I was unable to understand your answer. Please state the problem with which you would like help.

MARTIN   No more menu trees, okay.

VOICE FROM ABOVE   I'm sorry. I was unable—

MARTIN   Er—agent. Representative. *ELEVATE!!*

VOICE FROM ABOVE   (*Beat.*) You can't get more elevated than this.

MARTIN   I don't want menus! I just want some help without six lists of functions.

VOICE FROM ABOVE   I think you said, you want help with sexual dysfunction. Is this correct?

MARTIN   No!

VOICE FROM ABOVE   Okay, please restate your problem—

MARTIN   These menus are driving me crazy.

VOICE FROM ABOVE   I think you said, you are experiencing a mental illness. Is this correct?

MARTIN   No. My God! These menus are the most annoying thing on the planet.

VOICE FROM ABOVE   Duh.

MARTIN   I'm so . . . confused.

VOICE FROM ABOVE   We regret if the confusion is our fault. I am having difficulty understanding the problem with which you want help.

(MARTIN *paces, frustrated, perplexed.*)

MARTIN   My problem is—I forget what my problem is.

VOICE FROM ABOVE   I think you said, you no longer recall your problem. Is this correct?

MARTIN   Because it's taken so long to get this far —you know, just forget it. I'm done.

VOICE FROM ABOVE   I think you said you are finished—

MARTIN   Absolutely. Yes.

VOICE FROM ABOVE   Excellent. We are pleased to have been of service. Is there anything else we can help you with today?

MARTIN   NO! Yes. I don't know.

VOICE FROM ABOVE   Please wait at the end of this session for a personal message from God.

(*Hold music: seasonal, if appropriate.*)

(*Light Indian accent.*)

Hello, my name is Walter, and I have a brief message from the Lord thy God. To improve the quality of our service we request that you participate in a brief survey. Let's begin. Question one: was your prayer answered promptly and courteously . . . .

MARTIN   Aaargh!

(*Holding his head,* MARTIN *goes running out into the street.*)

NEW PHONE VOICE   Thank you. And how else can we provide you with a wonderful day?

(*As the liturgical MUSIC SWELLS—*)

(*Blackout.*)

END OF PLAY

THE PROBLEM WITH NEW YORK

Nicole Pandolfo

CHARACTERS

JEN: 20s/30s.
ASHLEY: 20s/30s.

TIME

Present day.

SETTING

A crowded bar at happy hour.

———————————

(*Lights up on a very crowded bar at happy hour.*)

JEN   The problem with New York is that I can't tell if I still love it here or if it's the worst.

ASHLEY   I know. I've been wondering that too lately . . . .

JEN   I can't believe we just waited a half an hour to stand at the bar.

ASHLEY   They should have special seating for women wearing three-inch heels.

JEN   I know right.

ASHLEY   It's the least they could do for that whole seventy-nine cents on the dollar thing.

JEN   The very least. By the way, those shoes are super cute.

ASHLEY   Thank you.

JEN   Are they comfortable?

ASHLEY   Actually, they are. Bloomingdales.

JEN   Nice.

ASHLEY   Oh no—I think I might have dated that guy over there back in college.

JEN   The cute one?

ASHLEY   No, the tall one standing next to him. He's such a jerk.

JEN   But he's tall . . . I wonder if he's available . . . .

ASHLEY   Quick, look away before he sees us.

(*They do.*)

ASHLEY   How's work going?

JEN   Another day, another bloodbath in print journalism . . . so . . . fine. It's going fine. You?

ASHLEY   I scored three times as many new clients at the agency this quarter than anyone else on my team, but my boss promoted Jared even though he emailed everyone a dick pic by accident last month . . . so it's going just fine too.

(*Beat.*)

JEN   Oh, I've been wanting to check out this new artisanal cheese curd restaurant on my block—want to go this weekend?

ASHLEY   Sure.

JEN   I read in *New York* magazine that this is the year for artisanal cheese curds.

ASHLEY   I think I saw that piece. Was it in the same issue as the profile on the seven-year-old tech trillionaire?

JEN   I think it was.

ASHLEY   Speaking of seven-year olds, maybe your nephew can show me how to use Snapchat sometime?

JEN   I'll ask if he can pencil you into his events calendar.

ASHLEY   Thanks. They're making us learn how to use it at work.

JEN   All this having to keep up with rapidly changing technologies to not lose your job is really making my skin dry out.

ASHLEY   Mine too. Maybe after our cheese curds on Saturday, we could try this new Tahitian spa in the Bronx that I heard about.

JEN   Tahitian spa?

ASHLEY   Yeah. Gwyneth Paltrow said they have the best rainforest animal fecal facials in all of New York City.

JEN   I think I read about that in *Harper's Bazaar*.

(*The girls both fling forward like they've been bumped into and spill their drinks.*)

ASHLEY   There goes seven bucks' worth of Grey Goose.

JEN   Honestly this city is too crowded.

ASHLEY   They need to put a cap on the amount of people allowed in at one time.

JEN   I wish there was a way we could force all the dilettantes to live in Staten Island.

ASHLEY   Or New Jersey at the least.

(*Beat.*)

JEN   Maybe we should move to New Jersey?

ASHLEY   That's a little dramatic isn't it?

JEN   I'm sick of it here.

ASHLEY   I know, but one plus is that you get to try a lot of great restaurants for free on Tinder dates.

JEN   Yeah but eating during an online date is kind of like eating during a job interview—no matter how good the food is, it's never that good.

ASHLEY   True. The whole time you're nervous and wondering if you've got peppercorn stuck between your teeth or if you're gonna get roofied when you go to the bathroom.

JEN   Or if things end up going really well then you're nervous if you're gonna get a UTI the next day.

Ashley   Like twenty-eight percent of my available anxiety-space is occupied by being worried about getting a UTI.

Jen   And it's so expensive here. This drink is happy-hour priced at $15. The happy-hour price is fifteen dollars.

Ashley   I know. These mozzarella sticks cost twelve bucks apiece.

Jen   That's thirty-six dollars on fried cheese.

Ashley   And that's half-priced.

Jen   This city is ridiculous.

Ashley   Alright, maybe we should move.

Jen   Definitely. Where should we move to? New Haven?

Ashley   New Haven? Ugh, have you ever met somebody who went to Yale?

Jen   Good point. Chicago?

Ashley   Too cold. Austin?

Jen   Too *Real World* season sixteen . . .

See, this is the problem with New York. New York sucks, but everywhere else sucks more.

(*Beat.*)

Ashley   To fifteen-dollar happy-hour martinis.

(*They clink glasses.*)

END OF PLAY

PROXIMITY

Kerri Kochanski

CHARACTERS

CLAIRE: Late 20s. Caucasian.
MARGARET: Late 20s. Asian-looking.

TIME

Now.

SETTING

The streets of America.

———————

(At rise, CLAIRE *walks on the street.* MARGARET, *a stranger, follows close behind. They continue to walk—crisscrossing the stage and forging new directions and paths. As* CLAIRE *walks, she becomes increasingly agitated by* MARGARET's *loud, clunky, intrusive footsteps. Finally, unable to take it anymore, she turns around—)*

CLAIRE   *STOP* following me . . .

(She turns back, resumes walking. MARGARET, *likewise, resumes walking. The footsteps begin to aggravate* CLAIRE *once again. Turning—)*

Look, I asked you nicely. So *PLEASE* . . .

(She resumes, then feels bad. Turning back—)

It's just that it's been a long day at work. A really *long* . . . So the *annoyance* of someone in my ear . . . "Click clock, click clock . . ."

(Grows annoyed just thinking about it.)

And the prox*imity* . . . .

(Looks MARGARET *over.)*

"Chinese" people like yourself—

See, I've *been* to China . . . I under*stand.* I know . . . People walk close to*gether* . . . 'Cause it's a big *country*, but there are too many *people* . . . Too many people crammed together. And so a big space becomes *small* . . . *Constricted* . . . .

(Suddenly realizing her surroundings, she throws out her arms.)

But here . . . ! Here in America we have space . . . !

(*She waves her arms about the space.* MARGARET *does not react.* CLAIRE *assumes* MARGARET *does not speak English. Therefore,* CLAIRE *begins to speak slowly, clearly, trying to make* MARGARET *understand—*)

The space is *big* . . . So you do not need . . . .

(*Gets frustrated.*)

Look, *ten steps* back . . . Do you think—do you think you could *just move* . . .

(*She measures out ten steps behind* MARGARET. MARGARET *does not react.*)

DO YOU UNDERSTAND? DO YOU UNDERSTAND ME . . . ? Or are you one of those people who speaks Chinese and doesn't know English—is learning English—some very *bad* English—some very bad—

(CLAIRE *begins to go off the deep end. She struggles to regain control. She looks at* MARGARET*'s feet. Refocusing—*)

Shoes . . . Because that's what I'm bothered by really. It's your *shoes*. . . .

(*Covers her ears.*)

They make *noise* . . . And it's not like I want to be this *mean person* . . . but . . .

(*Begins to wonder.*)

Why do you need shoes anyway? You're Chinese. Don't Chinese people not wear shoes . . . ? When I was over there—

(MARGARET *continues to stare.* CLAIRE *becomes disappointed.*)

You don't understand . . . .

(CLAIRE *points to* MARGARET*'s shoes, then puts her hand over her ears to demonstrate that* SHE (CLAIRE) *is bothered by* MARGARET*'s shoes. Then* CLAIRE *points behind* MARGARET, *indicating* MARGARET *should move back.* MARGARET *does not move.* CLAIRE *is very frustrated.*)

You don't understand . . . You *still* don't understand . . . .

(*Finally, overcome.*)

WHAT DO YOU WANT ME TO DO . . . ? TAKE *CHINESE* LESSONS . . . ?

(CLAIRE *is frazzled. Overpowered by her emotions, she becomes depressed. Gives up. Finally, after a while,* MARGARET *begins to speak—*)

MARGARET   (*American voice.*) You dropped your boarding pass . . . you were walking so fast, I couldn't reach you . . . I thought you might need it . . . might need your boarding pass . . . it says right here, you're due to fly out. Fly out this evening . . . .

Me, myself . . . I do fly sometimes . . . I flew over here . . . via London, transfer in Canada . . .

I live in Australia . . . Funny it must seem . . . I've been everywhere around the world. Mostly everywhere. Africa even. *Except* China . . . I'm a doctor . . . I don't have much time . . . but I did have time when I was a child growing up. A child growing up with a father who was in the army. Moving place to place.

An *American* father . . . .

(*Begins to reflect.*)

The things I've seen, the people I've known, the looks I have encountered . . .

(*Becomes disappointed. Then changes her focus, resuming.*)

You say that you don't like my shoes. . . .

(*Considers.*)

You don't have to like my shoes . . . You don't have to like *me*. . . . But I'm here. . . .

(*Proudly, standing her ground.*)

I am here. . . .

(CLAIRE *stands stunned.* MARGARET *notices, but continues.*)

Would you like your boarding pass . . . ?

(CLAIRE *accepts the pass. She continues to look at* MARGARET. MARGARET *indicates the pass.*)

They say it's warm in Morocco. . . . I don't know, I've never been. . . .

(*Hopeful, optimistic.*)

But I still would like—I still would like to go . . . to meet the people . . . see the types of things they think about. See what they like, what they do . . . *how* they live . . . why . . .

People are different . . . everywhere . . . they are different . . . in individual ways. . . .

(*Looks at watch.*)

It's time for my surgery . . . .

(*Correcting herself.*)

Not really mine, but—

CLAIRE   (*Surprised.*) You're a surgeon . . . .

MARGARET   (*Considering.*) Inside . . . inside people look the same . . . but some people survive, when others don't. . . . The same operation . . . operating and operating . . . until some people live, and others? They die. . . . Depends on the person . . . one person survives. . . . Another? She dies, under the glare . . . the *lights* in the examination room . . .

(CLAIRE *feels bad.*)

CLAIRE   I'm sorry . . . .

MARGARET   Your flight . . . .

(CLAIRE *self-consciously folds the crease on her pass.*)

CLAIRE   Yeah. . . .

(CLAIRE *continues to stand. Then*—)

After you . . . .

MARGARET   I'm going *this* way . . . .

(MARGARET *walks in the other direction.* CLAIRE *wishes her well*—)

Safe flight . . . .

(*CLAIRE feels guilty. She looks down at her shoes.*)

CLAIRE   Wait . . . !

>   (*She takes off a shoe. Holds it out to* MARGARET.)
>
>   Trade . . . ?

(MARGARET *isn't sure, but is willing.*)

MARGARET   What size . . . ?

(CLAIRE *is hopeful.*)

CLAIRE   Six—?

(MARGARET *kicks off her shoes.* CLAIRE *bends down and picks up* MARGARET'*s shoes. Then she puts her own in front of* MARGARET. CLAIRE, *excited, tries on* MARGARET'*s shoes, while* MARGARET *steps into* CLAIRE'*s.* MARGARET *has some difficulty putting on* CLAIRE'*s shoes.*)

MARGARET   I don't think they fit . . . .

CLAIRE   (*Disappointed, knowingly.*) No, of course they don't. . . .

(CLAIRE *moves to take off* MARGARET'*s shoes, but* MARGARET *stops her—*)

MARGARET   Keep them. . . . They're a friend of mine's . . . from India. . . . They'll be good for you. . . . Perhaps they'll soften your callouses. . . .

(MARGARET *begins to exit. She leaves* CLAIRE'*s shoes behind.* CLAIRE *is awestruck by* MARGARET'*s kindness.*)

CLAIRE   I don't even know your name. . . .

>   (MARGARET *exits.*)
>
>   I don't even—

(CLAIRE *looks down at her new shoes. She feels strangely inspired.*)

(*Blackout.*)

END OF PLAY

THE PSYCHICS' CONVENTION

John McKinney

The Psychics' Convention was first presented as part of an overnight writing challenge at Manhattan Theatre Source on MacDougall Street in New York City in 2007, and then further developed at the Workshop Theater in midtown in 2010. Since then it has been presented by various New York theater groups from 2011–2015.

Original cast:
SANDY: Sandy Yaklin
SONJA: Sonja O'Hara

Director: John McKinney

Workshop cast:
SANDY: Sue Wallach
SONJA: Sutton Crawford

Director: John McKinney

CHARACTERS

SANDY: 40s, conservative, well dressed, friendly with a slight maternal instinct toward her newfound young friend, SONJA.

SONJA: 16, lively, hip, edgy, fashionable with a dash of punk but not hard core. Mischievous and irreverent.

TIME

The present.

SETTING

A hotel lounge, late afternoon.

————————

(SANDY *and* SONJA *are sitting at a table, laughing. We pick up their dialogue mid-conversation. Their dialogue, however, is marked by odd pauses.*)

SANDY   The thing is . . .

(*Pause.*)

SONJA   Oh, right! I totally agree! I mean it's just like the minister in my church. . . .

(*Pause.*)

SANDY   Nooooo! He didn't!

SONJA   Oh! It gets much worse!

(*Pause.*)

SANDY   Eeeewww!
  (*Pause.*)
  Really?
  (*Pause.*)
  With a strap-on?

(SANDY *reacts to what is apparently a crude mental picture in her mind while* SONJA *projects her thoughts toward her and laughs.*)

SANDY   Eww! With the knobs and the spikes and—ooo, that's nasty! So then what happened? What? I'm sorry, I'm not getting that. I'm getting interference from the next table.

SONJA   Yeah, so am I. Seems like everyone's using telepathy in here.

SANDY   Well, I guess we'll just have to talk like normal people. So. Is this your first psychics' convention?

SONJA   Yup. You, too?

SANDY   Oh no. Been coming for years. By the way, my name's—

SONJA   Sandy! Pleased to meet you. I'm –

SANDY   Sonja! What a lovely name. So you're staying here at the hotel?

SONJA   Just got in yesterday, all the way from—

SANDY   Saginaw, Michigan? Really. I went to school in—

SONJA   Ann Arbor! No kidding! Which . . . is where you got your law degree!

SANDY   Yeah. I thought I was going to be a lawyer but—

SONJA   You ended up in law enforcement. Don't we all. Well, beats reading tea leaves.

SANDY   True. So. When did you first realize you had the gift?

SONJA   A few years ago. Though I don't know if I would call it a gift. Sometimes it can be a curse.

SANDY   (*Calling to waiter, offstage.*) Excuse me! Could I get a cappuccino, please? And—(*Pause.*)—a double latte for my friend? (*To* SONJA.) What do you mean, a curse?

SONJA   Well, sometimes hearing people's thoughts can really mess things up.

SANDY   Oh right, I know what you mean. I hear some of the things my boyfriend is thinking and I slap him right in the face. (*Laughs.*) He doesn't even know why!

SONJA   Yeah, well that same kinda thing happened to me last week. Only worse.

SANDY   How so?

SONJA   I found out my parents weren't my real parents at all.

SANDY   How horrible.

SONJA   Yeah. Turns out I was adopted. For years I could sense they were hiding some big secret from me, and little by little I was able to get inside their heads and figure out what it was.

SANDY   You know, you should be careful with that.

SONJA   Careful with what?

SANDY   Poking into people's private thoughts like that.

SONJA   Oh come on. What good is being a psychic if you can't uncover some juicy little secrets now and then?

SANDY   I'm not talking about everyday secrets like if somebody just masturbated. Actually, that's kinda fun! I'm talking about the kind of secret that's so shameful, it would tear people's lives apart if it ever got out. Almost everyone has at least one secret like that. When you start to get a whiff of one of those, you need to back off.

SONJA   Why are you telling me this?

SANDY   Because. I think there are some areas of people's lives that should remain private. Trust me, you start messing around with that and it's bound to backfire on you.

SONJA   No.

SANDY   No?

SONJA   That's not why you're telling me this. You're telling me this because you're afraid I'll find out *your* secret.

SANDY   Don't be ridiculous.

SONJA   I'm right, aren't I? Ha, I can feel you trying to scatter your thoughts right now. This must be a real whopper you're sitting on.

SANDY   Okay, I'm gonna warn you just once. Step off.

SONJA   I'm sensing embarrassment . . . a scandal of some kind. Wow, you were fired from your job . . . asked to leave your country club . . . whatever you did, this was a doozy!

SANDY   I'm warning you. Cut it out!!

SONJA   What was it? Embezzlement? Fraud? No wait. Something sexual. Maybe a little call girl action on the side?

SANDY   Alright, you want to play this game? Fine. Why don't you tell me the real reason you're here in town? Cause it's not the convention, is it? Ah . . . what's this? I see a . . . a birth certificate. The mother's name is filled in but not the father. You weren't adopted after all, were you? You grew up with your real mother, but you don't know who your father is. Ha! You're just an illegitimate little bastard daughter, is what you are. That's why you're here. You're looking for your deadbeat father! Your father who not only doesn't love you, but doesn't even know you exist! There. How's it feel?

SONJA   (*Crying.*) Fine! Okay! So we both have a secret past!

SANDY   (*Calm, sympathetic.*) Apparently so.

(*She hands* SONJA *a tissue.*)

So. You think your father's here? At this convention?

SONJA   I had a premonition he would be, yes.

SANDY   Makes sense. Psychic ability often runs in families. Did you check the hotel roster?

SONJA   Yeah, but there's no one here with a name like his.

SANDY   What is his name?

SONJA   Randy.

SANDY   Randy who?

SONJA   Randy Rickenmeyer.

SANDY   What?!

SONJA   Yep. Randy Rickenmeyer. I've been tracking him now for—

SANDY   Oh my god.

SONJA   What?

SANDY   OH MY GOD!

SONJA   You know him! Who is he??

SANDY   He's your father.

SONJA   I know that. Who is he really?!

(SONJA *slaps* SANDY *across the face.*)

SANDY   Alright. He's your mother.
   (SONJA *slaps her again.*)
   Your father!
   (*And again.*)
   Your mother!
   (*And again.*)
   Your father!
   (*And again.*)
   Your mother!
   (*And again.*)
   Your father!
   (*And again.*)
   (*Breaking down.*) HE'S YOUR MOTHER AND YOUR
   FATHER!!!! Randy Rickenmeyer is the name I used before my
   sex change operation!

(*Shock. Pause.*)

SONJA   Dad?

(*Blackout.*)

END OF PLAY

READ TO ME

Rebecca Gorman O'Neill

CHARACTERS

GRACE: 30s–60s (f), nicely dressed, perhaps an urban professional.
HANNAH: 20s (f), a young woman who works in a children's bookstore.

SETTING

A children's book shop. There is a "reading chair" and a few carpet squares for the children.

GRACE, nicely dressed, comes in, with a couple large tote bags of books. She plops herself down on the carpet, and looks expectantly at the reading chair.

HANNAH, who works here, might pass GRACE a few times, perhaps hoping she'll either make sense or go away. Finally:

HANNAH   Hi there.

GRACE   Hello.

HANNAH   Can I help you?

GRACE   Oh, I'm just waiting.

HANNAH   Waiting for someone?

GRACE   Waiting for story time.

HANNAH   There's not . . . not, today—are you with someone?

GRACE   I was told you'll read stories here—my niece brought her daughter here, and there was a nice man who read stories.

HANNAH   That's not today. . . .

GRACE   A policeman?

HANNAH   Yes, that's Officer Robbie, he comes in and reads to—

GRACE   Well, you can read, can't you?

HANNAH   Did you bring your niece's daughter? Or your . . . own. . . .

GRACE   I don't have children.

HANNAH   Ah.

GRACE   How does this usually work—do I pick something? I really don't want to have to—I always thought the reader picks.

HANNAH   I'm not the reader.

GRACE   Is there someone else—

HANNAH   It's just me.

GRACE   You could, though, do story time? I'm sorry, you do work here, right?

HANNAH   Yes, I work here—

GRACE   Good! You can read, then.

HANNAH   We do that for the really little kids.

GRACE   I'll be such a better audience than the little kids! I won't fidget or pick my nose or anything.

HANNAH   I should get back to the—

GRACE   Look, miss—

HANNAH   Hannah.

GRACE   Miss Hannah. I just want story time. I want someone to sit there, and I'll sit here, and I'll listen, and you read me a story.

HANNAH   Ma'am I'm sorry, I'm afraid you're a little confused.

GRACE   I don't see what the problem is—

HANNAH   Is there someone I can call?

GRACE   Of for heaven's sake I don't have dementia, I just want a story! Is that so much to ask?

HANNAH   We read the stories to the little ones who can't read yet. That's the whole thing. You can read, I'm guessing, and you're welcome to—

GRACE   That's the problem!

HANNAH   (*Why me?*) What's the problem?

GRACE   I can read. I can read, and read and (*She upends her bag to dump a pile of books.*) This is what I get. I'm (*insert age here*). I'm a good, educated woman, and I read the good books, the smart people books—*House of Leaves*, *Confederacy of Dunces*, *Gravity's Rainbow*. Have you ever—

HANNAH   Couldn't get through it.

GRACE   I know! So I gave that up, and decided, hey, let's read for fun, right? Some guilty pleasures—(*Holding up a book.*) This one's about a woman who gets sucked back in time to have steamy sex with a Scottish guy. (*Holding up a book.*) This one's about a woman who gets sucked back in time to have steamy sex with a vampire— she's a witch in the first place, so I guess—(*Holding up a book.*) and this one's set in Louisiana and there's vampires *and* werewolves—

HANNAH   I'm sorry, I get that you're frustrated, but what are you looking for?

GRACE   Anything. You can read. That will help me. Navigate. My life. I'm not a witch, or a vampire, or a whatever she—

HANNAH   I think she's a faerie.

GRACE   You've read this?

HANNAH   I watched the TV show.

GRACE   So you know what I mean? Just something simple and easy, and—

HANNAH   Okay, have you tried—

GRACE   I went to the young adult books, you know, teenagers are trying to figure out how to navigate their lives, right? So I'd find something to help me—but they're all about—

HANNAH   The apocalypse?

GRACE   Or the future. Or just trying to kill one another. In the future apocalypse.

Hannah   I'm sorry.

Grace   I tried *Twilight* but that was just—

Hannah   Sparkly vampires.

Grace   What on earth is anyone supposed to get from that?

Hannah   I don't know how we can help you, I mean, kids' books, that's not exactly going to help you navigate your life—you should try maybe—

Grace   Self help? *The Secret? The Seven Habits of Highly Effective People?*

Hannah   Well, if you've tried it all—

Grace   And you know what I stumbled across there in the self help section? Adult coloring books.

Hannah   Those are actually really—

Grace   Coloring books. The simple, easy focus of it all. Just thinking of it—so that's when I figured it out. What I was missing.

Hannah   Kids' books?

Grace   Youthful idealism. That's what I've lost. I've lost my youthful idealism and all I want, miss, All I need is . . .

Hannah   For someone to read to you.

Grace   Yes. Please?

Hannah   I don't see how that's going to help—

Grace   See this? (*The pile of books.*) I've been thinking too hard. Trying too hard. I need to try something easy.

Hannah   I wouldn't know what to pick. . . .

Grace   It doesn't matter what you pick. It just matters that I don't have to pick, that I don't have to decide something, or take care of something, or figure something out, or find the deeper meaning.

Please. I need to not have to, have to. Do me that kindness, and someday, if you're lucky, someone will do that kindness for you.

(HANNAH *looks at* GRACE. *Selects a book, and, in her very best reading voice begins . . .*)

HANNAH   Are you ready?

GRACE   What?

HANNAH   (*In her "reading voice."*) All right kids, it's reading time! Today we have a book about a very special little mouse. It's one of my favorites. Are you ready?

GRACE   I'm ready!!

HANNAH   (*Reading.*) If you give a mouse a cookie . . .

END OF PLAY

REALLY
REALLY REAL

Monica Flory

CHARACTERS

ONE: Any age, any gender.
TWO: Also any age, any gender.

TIME and SETTING

Really here, really now.

———————————

(*Lights up on two people,* ONE *and* TWO, *sitting on black theatre blocks or chairs.* ONE *and* TWO *may be of any gender, age, or race. They address the audience.*)

ONE   Look at us.

TWO   We're real.

ONE   Right here in front of you.

TWO   Talking to you.

ONE   Look at us!

TWO   Anyone care to smell us? I can prove that I really smoked a cigarette this morning.

ONE   I can prove that I really went to the gym.

TWO   You really didn't shower? Again?

ONE   I really didn't. My real name is (actor's real name).

TWO   Mine is Veronica.

ONE   Come on—really?

TWO   No, not really. It's (*actor's real name*).

ONE   Jerk.

(ONE *spits on* TWO.)

TWO   (*Offended.*) Disgusting!
    (*Then.*)
    Wanna see?

(*Shows audience the spit.*)

Real spit from this one's actual mouth!

ONE   You may be wondering if we're going to spend the whole five minutes this way. We're not.

TWO   We promise.

ONE   But in case you don't like what you see, you should know that we were selected from thousands of contestants.

TWO   I was selected for my hot bod and winning vocabulary.

ONE   I was chosen for my explosive temper.

(*Lunges at an audience member menacingly.*)

Hey—watch yourself!

(*Then, friendly, to the audience.*)

See? I could go off at any minute.

TWO   Do you want to see our audition pieces?

ONE   Wait—first let's let them see us really change costumes, live onstage.

TWO   Oooh—yes—good idea.

ONE   Watch this!

(*A costume-changing ritual, in which they show the audience their armpits, between their toes, etc. Ad lib dialogue. Perhaps there is music.*)

Okay, now we're ready to reenact our auditions. You go first.

TWO   Okay. I am as eccentric as humanly possible. I want you to know that I own a pet platypus and I rent out a porn star's walk-in closet. That porn star is my own mother, but I don't really like to talk about it, unless subtly coerced. My brother is a controversial professional athlete and I was an original member of Destiny's Child before they dumped me for Beyoncé. I have a lot of pain, but also sex appeal. Get a shot of my backside, will ya? That's one hot bod. Please visit my website at www dot hotbod—one word—dot com.

ONE   Nice. Very nice. Want to see mine?

Two   Of course they do.

One   My name is (*actor's real first name*). You want to know my last name?

(*Getting angry.*)

Isn't that a little personal? No, you tell me! You tell me your last name! Jones? Jones!?

(*Starts to cry.*)

I love you, man. I'm sorry about all that.

(*Angry again.*)

You are, too? What do you mean, you are too? That makes me want to . . . raise my voice and throw something! I mean, I am really angry here! I cannot control my emotions at all!

(*Friendly.*)

Thank you!

(*End of audition. Suddenly,* Two *starts kicking and punching in the direction of the audience.* One *joins in, enthusiastically.*)

Two   Wanna know what we're doing? We're . . .

One & Two   . . . breaking down the fourth wall!

Two   So we can get closer to you.

One   We want you to know what we are really, really like.

Two   (*Holds the hand of an audience member.*) Do you feel me?

One   (*Eats a crunchy apple close to another audience member.*) Do you hear that? Do you want a bite?

Two   Take a bite! It's a real apple!

One   Do you want to hear us sing?

Two   We can.

One   No, I know. Let's do something really, really together.

(One *lunges at* Two, *kissing* Two, *perhaps on the mouth.*)

Two (*After a beat.*) Whoa—I really felt something.

One I did, too.

(*A single rose appears, and* Two *takes it.*)

Two I could give you this rose.

One Am I special enough?

Two I don't know. I could give this to anyone.

One Please don't. I'm desperate.

Two I know you are.

One I'll do anything!

Two I know you will. Tell me, how do you feel right now?

One I need music.

(*This cues music to play.*)

I don't know—I never thought I could feel this way about someone I basically just met. But you're perfect! You're extraordinary! Give me that stupid flower!

Two Not unless you ask politely, with desperation.

One I want it! I want it! I want it! Please?

Two Do you really?

One Give it to me!

(*An elaborate fight. Music, grunting, yelling. Posing for selfies. Posing, smiling, then back to fighting. Rose petals fly. At the end of the fight,* Two *is lying on the floor as if passed out.*)

Very good. Now get up. What's wrong? Snugglebunny, wake up! Get up! I love you!! I'm sorry . . . .

(One *puts the mangled rose on top of* Two.)

(*Suddenly,* Two *springs up.*)

Two Did I fool you? For a second, maybe?

One Did you think any part of that was real?

Two   Did you believe us?

ONE   Please say yes . . . .

ONE & TWO   (*Increasingly desperate.*) Please say yes. Please say yes.
Please say yes.

(*As the lights fade on* ONE *and* TWO, *both beg the audience: "Please say
yes."*)

 END OF PLAY

SENT

Michael Edward Napier

CHARACTERS

BOBBY: 50.
ROBIN: 50, his wife.
JORDAN: Their son.

SETTING

A living room in a spacious apartment on the Upper West Side of Manhattan.

———————————

(BOBBY *sits at his desk staring at the computer screen.* ROBIN *enters.*)

ROBIN   (*Cheery. She sing-songs.*) H-e-l-l-o? Who wants a Pinkberry?

(*Silence.*)

BOBBY   (*Beat.*) Hi.

ROBIN   Where's Jordan?

BOBBY   He left.

ROBIN   Oh my God, what about his essay? It's due at midnight. He has to get that application in early, or he'll never get into Harvard.

BOBBY   That's what I told him. Then he said he didn't want to go to Harvard, and that Harvard was just like Collegiate.

ROBIN   That is just fucking ridiculous!

BOBBY   That's what I told him, too. Then I suggested Brown. He liked Brown. But he didn't like Providence. Even though he filled out the application. Because the truth is: He doesn't want to go to college at all. He wants to move to LA and try to get a TV show.

ROBIN   Oh, dear God! Wherever you are! What did I do to deserve this torment? You know, I can't leave the two of you alone together for twenty minutes! I mean, I've had fucking cancer, Robert.

BOBBY   Robin, come on!

ROBIN   It's true! I don't need this stress. What happened?

BOBBY   I said "none" was singular.

ROBIN   I beg your pardon.

BOBBY   I said "none" was singular.

ROBIN   Oh, Jesus Christ. We learned a rhyme in like the third grade: "None as well as neither and likewise with either—they singular be—though they seem to be three"—or something like that. How'd he miss that?

BOBBY   There are holes in the child's education. Gaping.

ROBIN   Well, frankly, you just helped him too much. Now, he feels helpless, so he resents you.

BOBBY   I had to help him, Robin.

ROBIN   Not to that extent. Excuse me, Bobby, what are you doing?

BOBBY   I'm tweaking his essay. What do you think I'm doing?

ROBIN   Is that the Common App?

BOBBY   Of course, it's the Common App. I know the codes and the passwords. Then I'm going to press send. The Harvard application's finished. He'll apply there early—if he doesn't get in, the Brown application'll be waiting in the dock.

ROBIN   Do you think this is ethical?

BOBBY   No. But I don't think the system is ethical. It's bullshit. Why is this any worse than paying twelve thousand dollars for SAT prep?

ROBIN   It wasn't twelve thousand dollars.

BOBBY   Yes, it was. I wrote the checks. It was slightly more actually. (*Reads.*) "None of the members of my family—IS—not are—particularly normal. Of course, I was only five when I realized I was the product of a mixed marriage—my Mom is Jewish, and my Dad is Christian—consequently, our Christmas tree always had a Star of David on top, and at every Seder, we always left the Prophet

Elijah a turkey breast sandwich on WASP white bread with mayonnaise and iceberg lettuce." See, it's good.

ROBIN   What? Are you kidding? It's brilliant. I can't believe he actually wrote it.

BOBBY   He has twenty-two words left. And just one little weave.

ROBIN   What?

BOBBY   Well, the whole essay is kind of a celebration of this multicultural community that is the building—and I want to add a little comment about Jerry and Zina since they represent an entire other generation—

ROBIN   Oh, OK. I see. I see that. I'm feelin' it.

BOBBY   Right? It's dimensionalizing. Just a very simple weave.
(*Types into computer.*)
OK. Now, we have the red diaper babies on six. Press save. We're done. (Beat.) And send.

ROBIN   Oh my God, Bobby! What did you just do?

BOBBY   I pressed Send.

ROBIN   You sent in his application? To Harvard? What if he does decide he'd rather go to Brown?

BOBBY   He's not going to do that, believe me.

ROBIN   Because he is going to be so pissed off that you did that. But at least, you did it, and thank God, it's over! IT'S OVER! IT'S OVER! IT'S OVER!

(*They give each other a high five.*)

ROBIN   (*She looks lovingly at him. Beat.*) OK. All right. Original or pomegranate? Pinkberry.

BOBBY   You know what? I'll walk on the wild side. Take the pomegranate.

ROBIN   You have to give me a bite, Bobby.

BOBBY   OK.

(*They eat their yogurts.*)

BOBBY   Wanta have sex?

ROBIN   Maybe after we finish our yogurts.

BOBBY   I meant after we finish our yogurts.

(*They continue to eat. The buzzer rings.* BOBBY *crosses to answer it.*)

BOBBY   (*Into the intercom.*) Hello?

JORDAN (**V.O.**)   Dad? I forgot my keys.

BOBBY   Shit!

JORDAN (**V.O.**)   Dad? I'm sorry. I got so angry before. It was stupid. I'm sorry. I'm just confused. OK? Between like Brown and Harvard? (*Beat.*) OK?

BOBBY   Yeah. OK. It's OK.

JORDAN (**V.O.**)   Could you buzz me in, please? I want to finish my essay and send it in. I've decided to apply early to Brown.

BOBBY   (*To* JORDAN.) Brown? Really? (*To* ROBIN.) OH MY GOD!

(*Blackout.*)

END OF PLAY

SHIPWRECKED

Adam Kraar

Shipwrecked was presented in June 2009 by Xoregos Performance Company at various venues around New York City. The play was directed by Shela Xoregos; original music was by James Barry. The cast was as follows:

JEANNE: Tracy Espiritu

TANAKA: Ralph Coppola

CHARACTERS

JEANNE: A young woman.
TANAKA: A young man.

TIME

The present.

PLACE

A remote, deserted island.

(*The beach, on a remote island. There is no sand, only stones.* TANAKA *pantomimes building a sandcastle. Then* JEANNE *enters.*)

JEANNE   What do you think you're doing?

TANAKA   I am building a sandcastle.

JEANNE   Have you lost your friggin' mind?

TANAKA   Look. This is the tower where the princess lives. I have built a special balcony, so the princess can watch the rising of the morning star.

JEANNE   Tanaka, for God's sake: for once in your life, could you try to be real?

TANAKA   I know this is very challenging and unpleasant for you.

JEANNE   Why do the sand flies only bite me?

TANAKA   It is better if you try not to scratch.

JEANNE   That's easy for you to say.

TANAKA   I have cooled this bottle in the ocean. Put it on the bites.

JEANNE   (*Taking the bottle and putting it on her bites.*) You coulda grabbed a roll of toilet paper, but no, you had rescue a bottle of sake.

TANAKA   We will drink it at sunset, no . . . ? The roar of the ocean will mingle—

JEANNE   Spare me—please.

(*Pause.* TANAKA *goes back to "building" his sandcastle.*)

JEANNE   Would you stop that. There's no sand on this whole godforsaken island!

(TANAKA *stops building.*)

JEANNE   And that so-called luxury yacht you bought?

TANAKA   I deeply regret certain errors of judgment.

(*This strikes* JEANNE *as so absurd that she laughs, not very kindly.*)

TANAKA   They told me it was top of the line. Clipper class, crafted from Portuguese cork, extremely yare.

JEANNE   When you saw that patch, the size of your big head, didn't you think—?

Do you ever think . . . ? "Yare"!

TANAKA   You will admit, 'til we passed Easter Island, the vessel was quite yare.

JEANNE   Look: there's part of the deck, sticking out of that reef.

TANAKA   Ah! Perhaps I can use that to support the main tower. (*Referring to his invisible sandcastle.*)

JEANNE   We are stuck here, with nothing to eat but coconuts.

TANAKA   If you like, you can nibble on my ear.

JEANNE   (*Exasperated:*) Ahhh!

(*After a moment,* TANAKA *resumes shaping the castle.*)

JEANNE   You know what my mother told me? If I kept going out with you, I'd lose my way. Ha—! I'm sorry, Mom. . . ! Coconuts! Coconut milk! Coconut tooth brush! Sick and tired of coo coo coo coo coconuts!

TANAKA   At the masked ball, they will serve us sushi.

(JEANNE *stares at him a moment, then for several seconds angrily kicks down the invisible castle.*)

TANAKA   Stop! Please! What are you doing?

JEANNE   . . . I'm going to the other side, see if I can find some shellfish.

TANAKA   You ruined your tower. . . . the front gate. The ballroom!

(*Pause.*)

JEANNE   Come on, Tanaka. Aren't you hungry?

TANAKA   It was so beautiful. The balcony defied gravity! And the ballroom was a circle of dreams. I was going to climb up the tower, on to your balcony, and then, as the sun slipped beneath the waves . . .

JEANNE   (*In spite of herself, somewhat crankily:*) . . . What?

TANAKA   We were going to dance in the ballroom. Spin and spin, like a star slowly rising.

   (*Admitting that the ballroom is gone:*)
   . . . Ha.

JEANNE   . . . I'm sorry.

TANAKA   No. You have every right—

JEANNE   It's just, you sometimes drive me nuts. Like these sand flies! Agh!

(TANAKA *takes the bottle and puts it on her new itch.*)

JEANNE   Jeezus! Agh. . . ! That helps, thanks. . . . I'm sorry about your "castle."

TANAKA   I have so much to learn. And I don't know if I want to learn it.

JEANNE   Well . . .

TANAKA   I so wanted to see you in your evening gown, glowing like the morning star.

JEANNE   Tanaka . . .

TANAKA   It was . . . so . . .

JEANNE   Yes, it was.

TANAKA   You mean . . . you saw it?

JEANNE   No. But, thank you for trying.

TANAKA   Well. It's gone now. I know it was never really there. . . . Let's go to the other side. I will kill the sand flies, and hunt for shellfish. And from the old deck I will build us a real roof. I know what is necessary. And I can do it.

(*Pause.*)

JEANNE   First, would you take me to the ballroom?

TANAKA   . . . Are you sure?

(JEANNE *nods.* TANAKA *leads her into an imaginary ballroom.*)

TANAKA   What do you think?

JEANNE   Awesome. The ceiling is big as the sky. And they're playing our song.

(JEANNE *lifts one of her arms, inviting him.* THEY *dance.*)

END OF PLAY

THE SPEAKER

Ellen Davis Sullivan

CHARACTERS

THE SPEAKER: Female, 50s–60s, Speaker of the House.
BREE: Female, 30–45, a capitol police officer just assigned to the Speaker.

TIME

A few minutes before the Speaker of the House is scheduled to address a political rally.

SETTING

A janitorial closet in a hotel hallway.

———————————

(BREE *pushes* THE SPEAKER *into the janitor's closet and follows her in. They're forced to stand very close.*)

THE SPEAKER   What's this?

BREE   Janitor's closet. It's safe for now.

(*Speaks softly into phone in her sleeve, too softly to be heard.*)

THE SPEAKER   What are you doing? What's going on? Is he out there?

BREE   They'll find him.

THE SPEAKER   You don't look concerned.

BREE   (*Doesn't speak.*)

THE SPEAKER   You don't answer questions?

BREE   That wasn't a question.

THE SPEAKER   So you do answer questions?

BREE   (*Shrugs.*)

THE SPEAKER   What do you know about him?

BREE   He's got a sign.

THE SPEAKER   And a pistol.

BREE   (*Gestures agreement.*)

THE SPEAKER   That doesn't worry you?

BREE   (*Shakes her head.*)

THE SPEAKER   You don't waste words.
(*Beat.*)
Has he done anything before?

BREE   He's armed. He's threatening to hurt you. That's all I know.

THE SPEAKER   You don't like me, do you?

BREE   (*Smiles.*)

THE SPEAKER   That was a question.

BREE   I just met you today. It's too soon to know.

THE SPEAKER   I'm guessing you don't much care for my politics. Most law enforcement types don't.

BREE   It's a step up to get assigned to the Speaker of the House.

THE SPEAKER   My husband Derek says they could have called me The Speaker even before I got the job . . . because of how much I talk. You know it's the way I got here, talking to people, persuading, telling my story.
(*Beat.*)
You probably like guarding pols you agree with.

BREE   It's not up to me.

THE SPEAKER   I don't mean to suggest you'd let someone kill me because you don't agree with my positions, it's just . . . .

BREE   You'd like to be protected by an anti-gun advocate?

THE SPEAKER   You don't think it would be smart to be guarded by a peacenik?

BREE   They set the terms of the engagement, not us.

THE SPEAKER   They?

BREE   The shooters. If they're armed, we have no choice.

THE SPEAKER   You'd kill someone for me?

BREE   I'm just like the last guy.

THE SPEAKER   Except he liked to talk. I got used to our conversations. Not that they were about anything, but it calmed me. I talk when I get nervous. Of course Derek would say I also talk when I'm not.

BREE   Are you nervous?

THE SPEAKER   A little. Except I can't see a guy with an idiotic slogan like "Keep the man in American" as other than crazy.

BREE   That doesn't mean he isn't dangerous.

THE SPEAKER   If I could just talk to him. I believe in words. You can change minds if you can talk to someone. He may need help. I could reach out to him—

(*Sound of footsteps thudding in the hall outside the door.* BREE *grabs the door knob and holds on.*)

BREE   Shhh!

THE SPEAKER   It doesn't lock? Some safe place.

> (BREE *extends her arm to hold* THE SPEAKER *back and keep her quiet. More footsteps, a pounding on doors.* BREE *braces herself to keep the door closed, but it's flung open.* BREE *gets in front of* THE SPEAKER *and shoots. The sound of several gunshots.* BREE *is hit and thrown to the ground.*)
>
> Oh, my god. Oh, my god. Are you . . . ?

BREE   I'll be OK.

(BREE *shows her Kevlar vest.*)

THE SPEAKER   And him?

BREE   I don't know.

(*Sounds outside the door include voices: "I've got his weapon" and "Call for a bus."*)

THE SPEAKER   Thank you. I can't . . . this is horrible. Is he going to live? Thank you for saving me—

BREE   Don't. Please don't.

THE SPEAKER   I . . . I . . .

BREE   Please.

(THE SPEAKER *goes to help* BREE *as she gets to her feet.*)

END OF PLAY

THAT THING THAT RINGS

Michele Markarian

That Thing that Rings premiered in June, 2013, by Screaming Media Productions as part of Gi60 Live US Edition at Brooklyn College, 2900 Bedford Avenue, in Brooklyn, New York, with the following cast and crew:

Director: Rose Burnett Bonczek

DEIRDRE: Samantha Fontana
JOHN: Schylar Westbrook
JIM: Mack Exilus

CHARACTERS

DEIRDRE: A twenty-something-year-old woman working in an office. She is dressed casually and wearing earbuds. She has an iPhone, from which she occasionally sends and receives text messages.

JOHN: A twenty-something-year-old man working in an office. He is dressed casually and wearing earbuds. He also has an iPhone, from which he occasionally sends and receives text messages.

JIM: A twenty-something-year-old man working in an office. He is dressed casually and wearing earbuds. He also has an iPhone, from which he occasionally sends and receives text messages.

TIME

The present.

SETTING

An office in Anywhere, USA. Three desks with chairs are set up, facing away from each other. All are equipped with a computer of some kind.

———————

(*At rise:* DEIRDRE, JOHN, *and* JIM, *each wearing earbuds, are seated at a desk, typing into laptops, occasionally picking up an iPhone to send or receive a text. Once in awhile one of them rocks to the music on their earbuds or drums on the desktop to the beat.*)

(*A telephone rings.* DEIRDRE *stops typing.*)

DEIRDRE   (*Taking earbud out of ear.*) Dude, is that your music?

JOHN   (*Continues typing.*)

DEIRDRE   I said, Dude, is that your music?

JOHN   (*Takes earbud out of ear.*) What?

DEIRDRE   That weird noise. Is that your music?

JOHN   I thought it was yours.

(DEIRDRE *and* JOHN *stare at* JIM. JIM *stops typing and takes off earbuds.*)

JIM   What?

JOHN   You hear that?

JIM   What is it?

DEIRDRE   Maybe some kind of fire drill?

(DEIRDRE, JOHN, *and* JIM *get up and start to look around the room. They stop at the phone and stare.*)

JIM   It's coming from that thing.

DEIRDRE   Oh my God!

JOHN   What?

DEIRDRE   It's—it's—one of those things you pick up and someone talks on the other end. Like on *Mad Men*.

JOHN   I've never watched it.

JIM   Oh. Yes! I've heard of these!
   (*To* DEIRDRE.)
   Pick it up.

DEIRDRE   What? No way! You pick it up!

JOHN   Don't look at me.

(JOHN *puts on his earbuds and starts typing.*)

JIM   You!

DEIRDRE   No, you!

JIM   You!

DEIRDRE   What if someone's on the other end?

JIM   Just do it.

DEIRDRE   What do I say?

JOHN   (*Takes off earbuds.*) Make that thing shut up, will you? I can't hear my music with that racket!

JIM   Go 'head.

(JIM *points his iPhone at* DEIRDRE.)

DEIRDRE   (*Picks up phone.*) Don Draper's office.

JIM   Cool!

(*Snaps* DEIRDRE'*s picture.*)

JOHN   Who's Don Draper?

DEIRDRE   (*Holding phone.*) They hung up.

JOHN   Good riddance.

JIM   I know, right? Who uses these weird, plugged in things, anyway?

(JIM *is fiddling with his iPhone.*)

DEIRDRE   What are you doing?

JIM   Posting the shot of you holding that thing.

(JIM *shows* DEIRDRE *the picture.*)

DEIRDRE   Cool! Totally retro!

(DEIRDRE *and* JIM *look at each other and stare.*)

JIM   Your eyes. They're blue. I never noticed it before.

(DEIRDRE *and* JIM *hold their gaze.*)

JOHN   (*Staring at* DEIRDRE *and* JIM.) You're freaking me out.

(*The telephone starts to ring again.* JIM *and* DEIRDRE *break free of each other's gaze;* JOHN *stops staring. One by one, they put their earbuds back on, ignoring the phone.* DEIRDRE, JIM, *and* JOHN *resume typing and texting as LIGHTS FADE.*)

END OF PLAY

TOO CLOSE
FOR COMFORT

Bruce Boeck

CHARACTERS

Ex: A girl, age –1 hour.
Wy: A boy, age –1 hour.

They are sitting very close together.

TIME

Five minutes from now.

_____

Wy   I don't want you to take this wrong, but I need my space. I think we should separate.

Ex   Oh my God, we've been together nine months, and you want to split up?

Wy   I just feel we should see others.

Ex   Are you seeing someone else?

Wy   No. There's no room for anyone else, silly! Where would we put them?

Ex   I know, we've been pretty close, I mean. Most of the time you've had your elbow in my ear, too. I'm glad you finally turned a bit.

Wy   Well, sorry, but it's not like there's any room here. I wish Mom had found us a bigger place, you know?

Ex   And with more to do. Frankly, it's become very boring here.

Wy   Yeah, wish Mom'd swallow a ball or something.

Ex   I admit, that trick of yours was fun, for a while.

Wy   Which one?

Ex   The one where we push our face against the wall? Mom always screams when we do that.

Wy   She gets so excited every time we move. She must be a cheap date.

Ex   Hey, that's our mom you're dissing! She's like our whole world, you know?

Wy   I know, I wasn't being critical. She just seems easily amused, you know?

Ex   I did like the music. The Mozart?

Wy   Boring. I preferred something with a beat, you know? Like at those aerobics classes Mom took?

Ex   Yeah, so you could boogie to it. THAT made Mom scream REAL loud!

Wy   I liked those classes, they got her blood going, there was a great beat. Until she said she got too fat. I blame you for that.

Ex   Me? Why are you blaming me? You're equally responsible!

Wy   I don't know, it just feels like I'm supposed to blame you for everything, you know?

Ex   Yeah, well, listen, bucko, don't think you're always gonna get away with it! Besides, Mom likes me best.

Wy   Nuh uh!

Ex   Uh huh! You notice how she always rubs MY side of the belly? And she likes that cool disco tunes like I do. It's got a great beat.

Wy   Well, percussion is easy when you have a metronome two inches above your head!

Ex   And does THAT ever get monotonous! Beat . . . beat . . . beat . . . beat . . . drives me crazy, sometimes.

Wy   I tried drawing on the walls, you know? Mom said it tickled, so I stopped. But I swear if I'm stuck here much longer I'm gonna teach myself to write!

Ex   Oh, she'd be so impressed! What are you going to write, your memoir?

Wy   Sure, why not?

Ex   What do you have to write about? "Chapter one: I was a bunch of icky goo, and then I looked like a chicken."

Wy   Look, it would be something like a work in progress, you know?

Ex   "Chapter two: I divided, a lot, then met my beautiful sister, whom I am trapped in this tiny room with forever, I think."

Wy   I don't think forever.

Ex   No? What makes you think that?

Wy   I don't know, just a feeling in my gut. But I'm not waiting. I'm busting out of this joint.

Ex   And how do you plan on doing that?

Wy   By putting my foot down.

Ex   Thanks, it was in my—

Wy   No, put your foot down, wiggle your toes. What do you feel?

Ex   There's a hole!

Wy   Our escape route. It's been getting bigger.

Ex   Oh wow! So finally we'll get out of here!

Wy   Thanks to me! I was stretching one day and felt something give way.

Ex   Um, where's the hole go?

Wy   Who cares? It's a way out. It can't be worse than being cooped up in here.

Ex   I wonder . . . I've heard Mom talking about a doctor visit—

Wy   Oh no, not another ultrasound! They make my ears ring!

Ex   What are you talking about, you always seem to have fun, waving, making faces, making crude gestures—

Wy   Mom loves those!

Ex Yeah, I know, but the doctor visits have been more often lately. Doctor has a nice voice, like Mom.

Wy It's getting kinda snug in here, you know?

Ex Yeah, like the walls are closing in.

Wy Do you hear voices? I mean, new ones?

Ex Well, there's Mom—and the doctor—but yeah, now that you mention it . . . whoa, what was that?

Wy I don't know, but look, all this fluid, it's draining out! We'll suffocate! There'll be nothing but air!

Ex The hole, we've got to get out!

Wy I'm pushing down. It's bigger, I might be able to crawl out.

Ex Don't leave me behind!

Wy No, I won't, just grab onto my—

Ex There's no room! You think we can turn around?

Wy If you do, you're gonna put your elbow in my ear. Again.

Ex I think if we turn around we can crawl out.

Wy Well hurry, the walls are really closing in now!

Ex OK I'll try. I'll go first, you push me, OK?

Wy Yeah, yeah, just hurry it up!

Ex OK, Here I goooooo! Wheeeeeeeee!

END OF PLAY

TRAIN

(FROM THE
TRANSIT PLAYS)

Sheila Callaghan

CHARACTERS

WALLACE AND JOE: Could be any age.

SETTING

A train.

Music. Suggestion of a train by ribbons and/or pieces of metal.

———————

(JOE *is walking down the aisle, carrying large heavy bags. He is overweight and dirty. The train jerks forward.* JOE *falls among his bags.* WALLACE, *seated nearby, glances up from his paper. He is well-ironed and prissy.*)

WALLACE   My eyes arrive on his sprawling melon body. He is completely unaware of his stench. He is repulsive.

JOE   Agggk.

WALLACE   And now he is now part of the floor. I suppose he wants me to help.

JOE   Help.

WALLACE   Defenses aligned . . . my coffee, my newspaper, my reading glasses, all rally against this putrid melon felled upon the train floor. He is not of my substance.

(*A black substance begins to leak out of the bag towards* WALLACE'S *shoe. It is tar.* WALLACE *does not see it.*)

JOE   My limbs are splayed, pointing like signposts . . . left leg toward Rahway, right leg toward Elizabeth, back to hell and belly to God. He crawls into his paper.

WALLACE   I crawl into my paper.

JOE   But he doesn't know THIS . . . I've got a suitcase full of tar. And another full of flight. Tar or feathers, which will be his fate?

(JOE *extends his hand to* WALLACE. WALLACE *ignores it enthusiastically.*)

WALLACE   My oh my, what an interesting assortment of ink and pulp before me. I can't possibly disengage myself from it long enough to glance at the melon hand.

(WALLACE *crosses his ankles at* JOE.)

JOE   His stockings are torn. His soles are worn. He plays money on his instrument but the tune is one of lack lack lack. He is of my substance.

WALLACE   Still looking at me . . . I feel a bend of my frontal lobe . . . and in my mouth . . . the acid of guilt.

JOE   My arm is broken.

WALLACE   If it were my mother. If it were my dog. Or me. Is it me? No, no. But . . .

JOE   My waist is broken. And my arm.

WALLACE   My guilt is mutinous in my mouth. Crisis.

JOE   The tar creeps closer to his shabby wingtips . . . oooh, he's gonna get it . . . ruined shoes then late to work then angry boss, unemployment, mutilated self-esteem, revolted offspring, adulterous spouse. . . .

WALLACE   Oh . . . FINE! I shall aid the melon man.

(*With great fanfare*, WALLACE *extends his hand toward* JOE*'s. They touch. They freeze.*)

JOE   Too late!

   (*Sound of a train whistle outside, then an ambulance siren, then a cooing pigeon.*)

   Pigeon flies from other suitcase, eats man's eyes for lunch.

(*A pigeon flies from one of* JOE*'s suitcases and gouges* WALLACE*'s eyes.*)

WALLACE   No eyes! And my feet are peanut-buttered to the floor!

JOE   He waited one whistle too long . . . .

WALLACE   Eyes gone . . . shoes ruined . . . lost job, adulterous wife. . . .

(WALLACE *pitches forward, lands on top of* JOE.)

JOE   Oof!

WALLACE   And now, nose first into the melon body. Stink cloud rises from the friction. Smell of pepper, of lime, of wet cement and Fresca and zoo turtles and cheddar.

JOE   We are one.

(JOE *and* WALLACE *sing a tune together in unison.*)

WALLACE AND JOE   We are one
We are one
Hmmmmm

JOE   And a moral to the story, as if every hole demands a cork.

WALLACE   I should have helped him sooner . . . but something in his smell sang of inevitability, as though my nose had been poised at his spongy heart since the day I earned my face.

   (*An awkward silence.*)

   So.

JOE   So.

(JOE *makes some clicking noises with his throat.*)

WALLACE   What was that?

JOE   What?

WALLACE   I felt a ripple in your thorax.

JOE   I'm swallowing a percussive cadence to welcome you to my mass.

WALLACE   Oh.

JOE   I'm Joe.

WALLACE   I'm Wallace.

JOE   A pleasure.

WALLACE   Yes.

(*A beat.*)

I suppose we're both the floor now.

JOE   We are. We will lie wise and long beneath countless pairs of shuffling wingtips across the vast eternities of transit. It might be beautiful, you know.

WALLACE   I can't smell your smell any more . . . .

JOE   Maybe you've stopped trying so hard.

WALLACE   Maybe.

(*A beat.*)

JOE   Hey. Guess what?

WALLACE   What?

JOE   My affliction is broken.

(*A beat.*)

WALLACE   Mine too.

(*The tar consumes them both and they become the floor. The pigeon pecks at them. Then flies off.*)

END OF PLAY

TWO COUSINS FISHING AFTER A REHEARSAL DINNER AT A LESBIAN WEDDING

Steve DiUbaldo

The original production of this play was in New York City with
the Middle Voice Theater Company at Rattlestick Playwrights
Theater for the Speechless: Play in a Day Festival.

Original Cast:
MAGGIE: Catya McMullen
LOUIE: Victor Cervantes Jr.

Directed by Ren Dara Santiago.

CHARACTERS

MAGGIE: 20s. Female. She likes anime and making ironic parkour videos.

LOUIE: 20s. Male. He uses Grindr in public bathrooms to locate potential blowjobs.

They both have some intimacy issues.

TIME

A humid summer night. Tomorrow is the wedding.

SETTING

A dock where LOUIE and MAGGIE like to go fishing.

_____

(MAGGIE *and* LOUIE *are drinking and fishing on a dock. There's a cooler nearby.*)

MAGGIE   "Babe."

LOUIE   "Babe."

MAGGIE   "I love you, Babe."

LOUIE   "Aww. Babe."

MAGGIE   "Baby, make a toast."

LOUIE   "Babe, you're embarrassing me."

MAGGIE   "Oh my God, Babe. (*Crazy angry.*) DO IT!"

(*They crack up. Deep breath "ahh's" at the end of the laughter.*)

LOUIE   I usually wait 'til the wedding to throw up, like never the rehearsal dinner.

MAGGIE   Dude, JoEllen is the type of chick who has to be the source of others people's happiness or else she's a bitter like *gash* of a human.

LOUIE   Fishing with you always gets so real.

MAGGIE   And she always does that thing where she smiles at you . . . like . . . "Louie. Oh, Louie." Like she really believes she can read your mind or like see in your soul or something.

LOUIE   I went fishing with her last week and she had this big bite that was actually just weeds but the line snapped and she went flying backwards . . . and this bitch freaked out and jumped in the lake and went swimming after the fish. A non-existent fish. She's nice, though.

MAGGIE   Yeah, she's nice when she's in control.

LOUIE   Do you think she controls Vanessa?

MAGGIE   JoEllen? Are you asking me if you think I think JoEllen controls my sister?

LOUIE   "Oh my God, Babe! Babe! (*Crazy angry.*) MAKE THE TOAST!"

MAGGIE   Stoked on my new in-law. Stoked. Like Vanessa is some prize though . . . .

LOUIE   Vanessa is such a fact parrot, it makes me sick.

MAGGIE   I know, oh my God I KNOW . . . I told her at breakfast the other day something like . . . hey ya know buttermilk? It doesn't even have butter in it. And she'll just sit there, all stonefaced, because she's not interested in any conversation where she's not a master of the topic . . . and then days later, we'll be at breakfast eating pancakes, and she's like—

LOUIE   "Hey, ya know buttermilk? It doesn't even have butter in it."

MAGGIE   You're my favorite cousin because you get it, ya know, you get it.

LOUIE   We come from a long line of fact parrots.

MAGGIE   This is gonna be some lesbian wedding tomorrow. I'll go from little social circle to little social circle at the reception and get told the same thing eight hundred times.

LOUIE "The Netherlands is the first country to implement gay marriage, ya know."

MAGGIE No way! That is an amazing fact! Especially for a straight person to know! Oh my God, like all the straight people here are either wildly uncomfortable or super proud of themselves for not being uncomfortable in the presence of gay love.

LOUIE Is Robert coming?

MAGGIE Robert my first boyfriend Robert? I have no idea. God, I hope not. Random . . . .

LOUIE No I was just—When we were in health class in middle school, the teacher showed us a map of the male body and the dick was ya know, like average-sized and everyone was asking about it, and the teacher was finally like, *yes five to six inches is average*. Robert was never the same after that.

MAGGIE Because he had a small dick?

LOUIE No, it's like, disturbing massive. You never saw it?

MAGGIE I was like, eleven. Wait. Did *you* see it?

LOUIE Yeah, he's a total closet case.

MAGGIE Robert?

LOUIE Yup. He gave me head while we watched *Entourage* in his grandma's basement.

MAGGIE Ew.

LOUIE He said we could never talk about it, that he was doing it for the experience.

MAGGIE How many "experiences" did you have with him?

LOUIE I mean . . . we watched a lot of *Entourage*.

MAGGIE God.

LOUIE Oh come on, Maggie. You're totally that girl whose first boyfriend was gay. What do you complain about when you complain about men? They're not sensitive enough and they don't like the things you like. I'm not saying that loving anime and making ironic parkour videos are homosexual activities, because obviously they're just weird, but . . . you get pissed because the guys you date won't even try to understand it.

MAGGIE   At least I don't try to find "romance" on Grindr while I'm taking a dump.

LOUIE   Why you gotta talk shit?

MAGGIE   I'm not talking shit, I'm just saying. If I had the option to get a sloppy beej in a public bathroom twenty-four hours a day maybe I wouldn't spend so much time worrying about real intimacy and I could become a ho bag like you.

(MAGGIE *smiles and looks into* LOUIE's *soul.*)

LOUIE   Why are you looking at me like that?

MAGGIE   Louie. You are so insecure, Louie.

LOUIE   I feel like I can tell you this because we're close, ya know, we're close.

MAGGIE   Are you gonna make this real right now? You are . . . .

LOUIE   You're one of those people that does all the shit that pisses you off about everyone else.

(LOUIE *goes to the cooler and grabs two beers.*)

MAGGIE   Will you get me some water? I'm parched.

(LOUIE *keeps a beer for himself and puts* MAGGIE's *back. He puts some ice in a cup and gives it to* MAGGIE.)

LOUIE   Here. Make your own water.

MAGGIE   That's my joke.

LOUIE   It is not.

MAGGIE   Give 'em ice in a cup—"make your own water." That's my joke.

(*A pause. They fish for a while.* MAGGIE *munches some ice from her cup. It's annoying.*)

I love you.

LOUIE   Fish.

(*A pause. Ice munching. Fishing.*)

I love you too.

(*Lights.*)

END OF PLAY

TWO WOMEN AND A DEER

Graham Techler

CHARACTERS

FRAN: A woman, could be any age.
PEGGY: A woman, could be any age.

TIME

Whenever.

SETTING

I-90 West between Detroit and Chicago.

NOTE

The car can and should be as simple as two rolling chairs. The Body of a Deer, either played by two people in a deer costume like in that weird F. Scott Fitzgerald short story, or by a big prop deer.

(FRAN *drives.* PEGGY *rides shotgun. Long pause.*)

FRAN   Would you rather . . . ?

PEGGY   Mhmm?

FRAN   Okay, this is all option one. Option one: This ride is . . . thirty hours long. And we can't ever pull over or stop driving or sleep. We're constantly shitting and farting and—

PEGGY   Constantly?

FRAN   Whenever it comes up.

PEGGY   And why can't we sleep?

(FRAN *thinks.*)

FRAN   Because I'm doing this.

(FRAN *drifts off to the side of the road and drives over the bumps. Then drives back.*)

FRAN   The whole time.

PEGGY   Okay. Or?

FRAN   Or, the drive is still about four hours. We can sleep and take as many breaks as we want. But every time we pass a piece of roadkill, it appears in the car.

PEGGY   We pull over and . . . pick it up?

FRAN   Nope, we pass it and it materializes in the car.

PEGGY   Okay.

(*Pause.*)

FRAN   I'll remind you that so for we've passed about five or six full-sized, partially liquified deer carcasses.

PEGGY   Yes. Is there a limit on the number based on space?

FRAN   No. We have to make room.

PEGGY   Can we use the trunk?

FRAN   No.

PEGGY   Okay.

FRAN   So. Thirty hours. No breaks. Shitting.

(*She drifts over the bumps.*)

FRAN   Or the road kill.

PEGGY   Alright.

(*Pause.*)

FRAN   *Thirty hours . . . Roadkill.*

(*Looong pause.*)

PEGGY   Mmmm. Roadkill.

FRAN   Me too.

(*Later.* PEGGY *drives.*)

PEGGY   D my name is D'Angelo, my wife's name is Dominique, we live on Dagobah, and we sell danger!

FRAN   E my name is Eskimo, my wife is also an Eskimo, we live in Engleton, and we sell eels!

PEGGY   F my name is Fran, my wife's name is Fortinbras, we live in Flevinshire, and we sell forty bottles of beer on the wall, forty bottles of bee—!

FRAN   G my name is Ginger, my husband's name is Gargamel, we live in Grea—grand . . . Gr—shit.

PEGGY   H my name is Helios, my wife's name is Helga, we live in Hell on Earth, and we sell hemorrhoids!

(*Later.* PEGGY *and* FRAN *stand on either side of the car. They've just hit a big ol' DEER.* PEGGY *cries.*)

PEGGY   I didn't mean to! I didn't mean to!

FRAN   It's okay . . . It's okay . . . It happens. . . .

PEGGY   I know it happens! I didn't mean to!

FRAN   No one ever does! No one ever means to smash their car into a deer and kill it. And even then no one ever means to not kill it instantly, so it sits there bleeding out for a full half hour. No one ever means that, baby.

PEGGY   I never mean to!

FRAN   How do you mean?

PEGGY   I never mean to kill deer.

FRAN   . . . Naturally.

PEGGY   But it happens.

FRAN   Of course . . . This isn't the first time?

PEGGY   Oh no. I've killed a lot of deer . . . s. I don't know why.

FRAN   That's horrible. It destroyed the car.

PEGGY   I've had a lot of cars.

FRAN   I can't believe you've never mentioned it.

PEGGY   Yeah . . . Well . . . I can't believe I've killed so many deer.

(*Later.* PEGGY *and* FRAN *sit on either side of the DEER.* FRAN *reads* PEGGY*'s tarot on the DEER.*)

PEGGY   Well? What does it say?

FRAN   The Four of Cups. The moment is now to make a great atonement.

(PEGGY *cries.*)

PEGGY   But how?! I'm sorry. This is crazy. This is a mistake. Let's get on the road.

FRAN   Peggy, grab a book out of the car.

PEGGY   What book?

FRAN   Any book. I don't have a Bible or the Heptameron. So any one will—

(PEGGY *pulls a pamphlet out of her jacket.*)

PEGGY   What about this pamphlet on *Ten Guideposts for Healthy Cuticles*?

FRAN   . . . That'll do.

  (FRAN *takes it and rubs it.*)
  (*Intones.*)
  GAHH DO FURIO MAGICK-A NOSTRO!
  FUTONO BASHI ORGONO!
  (*To* PEGGY.)
  Put your hands on the deer.

PEGGY   Do I have to?

(FRAN *gives her a look.* PEGGY *places her hands on the deer's head*.)

FRAN   SHANA FOSTRONI! OCCUL MARONI!
  SHEENO! SHEENO FOTARUNA!
  (*To* PEGGY.)
  Now you say that part.

PEGGY   Sheeno . . . Sheeno fotaruna . . .

(*Pause.*)

FRAN   Well, that's that. I've never had to exorcise the spirits of so many deer. But I think it worked.

PEGGY   Do we have to bury it now?

FRAN   I think it likes it out here, Peg.

PEGGY   . . . Thanks Fran. Bye, deer.

FRAN   Bye, deer.

(*They get back in the car. As they drive away . . .*)

PEGGY   A my name is Achilles, my wife is Agatha Christie, we live in the Andersonville prison, and we sell apples!

(*Lights fade.*)

END OF PLAY

UP ON A ROOF

Scott C. Sickles

CHARACTERS

HAL: Quirky in a way not everyone finds cute; unconfident and straight-laced but pleasant.

GEMMA: Flirty and confident; beautiful; has hidden depths that surprise even her.

ROBBIE: Big, handsome, and athletic; a nice enough guy

TIME

A cool, clear night.

SETTING

An apartment rooftop on a clear, cool night.

NOTE

The characters can be any age, but early twenties through mid-thirties makes the most sense. While the characters faintly hear music, it's written to be imagined by the audience. If the production wishes to play music, that's fine: it should be quite low and there should be a tango at the appropriate spot.

(*At rise:* HAL, *a straight-laced but pleasant guy, takes in the view. He takes in a deep breath and lets it out, relaxing and at peace. As he takes a sip of his beer [in a plastic cup],* GEMMA *enters. She's very pretty, confident and flirty, but not at all slutty or sloppy. She's glad to see him.*)

GEMMA   There he is.

HAL   Hey, Gemma.

GEMMA   Beautiful night.

HAL   Can't argue with that.

GEMMA   (*Takes in music [unheard by the audience].*) Hear that?

HAL   Just barely. Is that a . . . ?

GEMMA   Tango.
    (*Looks him over, works up her nerve.*)
    Dance with me, Hal.

Hal   Oh . . . I don't dance.

Gemma   Lucky for you, I'm a great teacher. I even taught Robbie.
(*Sensing his shyness, gently takes his arm.* Hal *wordlessly, bashfully, declines. She smiles through her disappointment.*)
If you're not going to dance, at least let me have a hit of your beer.

(Gemma *takes his cup and pulls a sip. Before he can object, the beer sticks in her throat. She swallows it, scowling.*)

Hal   It's non-alcoholic.

Gemma   Great. The drink of choice for people who hate fun but love to pee.
(*Grows apologetic when* Hal *turns away, blushing and smiling.*)
Does that bother you? When I say things like that? Because, you know, I don't—

Hal   You're fine.

Gemma   Really? Fine? Hm. Because some would say I'm spectacular.

Hal   (*Smiling.*) I'm sure they would.

Gemma   Or compelling. Even mesmerizing.

Hal   All too true. Robbie's very lucky to have you.

Gemma   He certainly is.

Hal   Very lucky.

Gemma   What if he didn't, you know . . . "have me?"
(*Meeting* Hal*'s deer-in-headlights look.*)
Don't get me wrong. Robbie's great.

Hal   He's the best.

Gemma   None better. It's just sometimes . . . Sometimes, I wish I met you first.

(Gemma *puts her hand on* Hal*'s. They stare a moment, then* Robbie, *their age; handsome and athletic, enters.*)

ROBBIE   (*Mock angry.*) Hey! You trying to steal my girl?

HAL   (*Sadly, to* GEMMA:) Wouldn't dream of it.

ROBBIE   (*Gives* HAL *a bro-hug.*) That's what makes you the World's Greatest Wingman.

(*Puts his arm around* GEMMA.)

Not that I need a wingman anymore.

GEMMA   Robbie, your BFF here is totally lame. He refused to dance with me.

ROBBIE   Dude, you don't know what you're missing. Here:

(*Humming a tune, leads* GEMMA *though a couple of swing moves. To* HAL:)

Not bad, huh?

(ROBBIE *dips her; pulls her to her feet.* HAL *forces a smile and claps.* ROBBIE *takes a bow, not noticing* GEMMA *looking at* HAL, *wishing she was with him instead.*)

ROBBIE   You guys are missing the party. Come on back inside.

GEMMA   Go ahead. I'll be there in a second.

ROBBIE   Just one, okay?

(*Nuzzles her. To* HAL:)

Isn't she the best?

(HAL *nods.* ROBBIE *exits. After a moment,* GEMMA *crosses to* HAL. *Before he can speak, she gives him a gentle but firm kiss. Pause.*)

GEMMA   I just wanted to know what I was missing.

(HAL *watches as* GEMMA *hurries to the exit. At the last moment, she stops and looks back. They start at each other, longingly.*)

(*Blackout.*)

END OF PLAY

A VERY SHORT PLAY ABOUT THE VERY SHORT PRESIDENCY OF WILLIAM HENRY HARRISON

Jonathan Yukich

CHARACTERS

WILLIAM HENRY HARRISON: Ninth President of the United States.
SULLY: His devoted assistant.

TIME

The year is 1841.

SETTING

The President's White House chambers. Keep it simple: desk, bed, a few chairs.

The Presidency: Day 1

(*Lights up.*)

HARRISON   I showed them, eh Sully!

SULLY   To be sure, sir!

HARRISON   How long was my speech?

SULLY   Nearly two hours—the longest in American history!

HARRISON   In the pouring rain, no less! And they said I was too old and frail to be president!

SULLY   What do they know!

HARRISON   Naysayers! Every last one of them! I haven't felt this alive since Tippecanoe! When do we get started on the nation's business?

SULLY   As soon as we get you out of these wet clothes.

HARRISON   No time, Sully! Damp clothes be damned! Full speed ahead! Let's set the agenda!

SULLY   Your can-do attitude is electrifying, sir. It's going to be a presidency for the ages!

HARRISON   A-a-a-a-ACHOO!

(*Pause. The two men look at each other, ominously. Blackout.*)

The Presidency: Day 2

(*Lights up.*)

Harrison   Sully, it's the second day of my administration. What shall we get to work on? Let's go big, aim high!

Sully   Well, there's the issue of revenue tariffs, or the cash-strapped treasury, or the escalating crisis between slave states and free states.

Harrison   Perhaps I'll write a few letters first. To family and friends.

Sully   How are you feeling, sir?

Harrison   Just dandy, except for the bowl of phlegm I coughed up this morning. It had a purplish hue. I had the maid save it so you could see yourself.

Sully   Splendid.

Harrison   But it's nothing a cup of hard cider can't cure, eh Sully, my boy!

(*Blackout.*)

The Presidency: Day 7

(*Lights up.* Harrison *gradually appears sicklier.*)

Harrison   Being president is more tiresome than I imagined. I'm constantly beset by office seekers. It's impossible to get anything meaningful done. I thought I would be a trailblazing figure, one who would usher in a long era of Whig Party rule. Instead, I feel like a fat puppet. I can't seem to get my head above water.

Sully   The challenges are legion, sir.

Harrison   And on top of it all, I've started bleeding from my rectum. It's probably just allergies.

(Sully *looks on, dismayed. Blackout.*)

The Presidency: Day 11

(*Lights up.*)

SULLY   Mr. President, we should prepare for your cabinet meeting.

HARRISON   (*Becoming more and more erratic, reflective, and deflated.*) Sully, did I ever tell you about the time I met Tecumseh?

SULLY   On several occasions.

HARRISON   What a son-of-a-bitch that guy was. He tried to kill me, you know. Came at me with a hatchet. Said that I hornswoggled tribal leaders into taking a bad deal. Of course, he didn't use the word hornswoggle—he had some fancy words—

SULLY   (*Quoting Tecumseh with a hint of admiration.*) "No tribe has the right to sell land, even to each other, much less to strangers. Sell a country! Why not sell the air, the great sea, as well as the earth. Didn't the Great Spirit make them all for the use of his children?" Are those the words you mean?

HARRISON   Some such silliness. I'll have you know, the treaty he so opposed granted our nation over three million acres of land. Who is he to question its merit? I'm glad to say he met his end in 1812. Let that be a lesson to those who interfere with American destiny.

(*Pause. A grimace of consternation, perhaps with a feeble groan.*)

Sully, I believe I've just soiled my pants.

SULLY   Number one or number two, sir?

HARRISON   Honestly, I couldn't say.

(*Blackout.*)

The Presidency: Day 18

(*Lights up.*)

HARRISON   Where's Anna!

SULLY   If you'll recall, sir, the First Lady stayed behind in North Bend. She won't be here until the spring.

Harrison   I do miss her so.

Sully   You don't look well, sir. Perhaps we should get you to bed?

Harrison   Nonsense. I'm fighting fit! Why in hell would you suggest I go to bed?

Sully   Your eyes are bloodshot, your flatulence is chronic, and there are lymph nodes visibly growing on your neck. Also, you've been speaking in Latin and claiming you're Cicero. I think it's possible you may have a fever.

Harrison   Oh, so you're a doctor now, Sully?

Sully   No, sir. I just think that, though you are a robust 68 years of age, perhaps, in hindsight, it wasn't a good idea to give a two-hour speech in the freezing rain.

Harrison   I see. You're fired.

(*Blackout.*)

The Presidency: Day 23

(*Lights up.*)

Harrison   Sully, I'm sorry I fired you.

Sully   You were entirely justified, sir.

Harrison   I've been lost without you these last few days.

Sully   It's all in the past now. Shall we attend to the nation's business?

Harrison   Perhaps a power nap first?

Sully   Excellent idea. Sir, I don't mean to offend, but are you still feeling well?

Harrison   Infinitely well!

Sully   Are you lying?

Harrison   Yes.

(*Blackout.*)

The Presidency: Day 29

(*Lights up. A decidedly diminished, weakened* HARRISON *is now in bed.*)

HARRISON   Sully, what have the doctors said to you?

SULLY   That you are stricken with an awful cold, and that you'll be on your feet in no time.

HARRISON   Yes, that's what they say, but what do they mean?

SULLY   Shouldn't we take them at their word?

HARRISON   It can't be easy to tell a President that he is dying.

SULLY   No one has said anything about dying.

HARRISON   Yes, but everyone is thinking it—including you, Sully.

SULLY   Why, sir, I never—

HARRISON   Do you belittle me with false optimism? I'd rather you not treat me like a child. Tell me, who shall take over when I'm gone?

SULLY   I assume the Vice President.

HARRISON   Tyler? John Tyler? But he's the biggest son of a bitch of them all!

SULLY   Then why did you select him?

HARRISON   For the same reason anyone selects a Vice President— to win!

SULLY   I'm fairly sure it's written somewhere that the Vice President assumes the Presidency.

HARRISON   Well shit. Our nation has so much to figure out.

(*Blackout.*)

The Presidency: Day 32

(*Lights up.*)

HARRISON   This is it, Sully, I'm fading. My final hour, I can feel it. How many days have I been president?

SULLY   Thirty-two, sir.

HARRISON   (*Lamenting.*) Is that all? Oh dear. I'll be the first to die in office.

SULLY   It was bound to happen at some point.

HARRISON   And Anna will be the only First Lady to never see the White House.

SULLY   This will save her a trip.

HARRISON   Oh, history will make a laughingstock out of me.

SULLY   You don't know that for sure, sir. Perhaps another president will come along and only survive thirty-one days in office. Then no one will remember you.

HARRISON   We can only hope. Oh, I could have accomplished so much, if I'd only had the time!

SULLY   And the ideas, and the vision.

HARRISON   Those too. It's possible that one day historians will resuscitate my legacy. Oh, in my final moments, let me believe this! May they one day celebrate my promise! May they praise my untapped greatness! May they even write a play about me!

SULLY   I suppose anything's possible, sir. But it would have to be a very short play.

(*Blackout.*)

END OF PLAY

WEAKNESSES AVAILABLE UPON REQUEST

Earl T. Roske

CHARACTERS

BRICKYARD: Superhero, big, 50s.
SHARK: Superhero, thin, 30s.

_____

(*Lights up on a superhero corporate office.*)

BRICKYARD   Come in, come in. Have a seat please.

SHARK   Great, thanks. Here?

BRICKYARD   That'll do.

SHARK   Thank you.

BRICKYARD   So, we've been going over your resume here at Task Force Ten, and we're quite impressed.

SHARK   Gosh, thanks. Truthfully, I was beginning to think I'd never hear from you guys.

BRICKYARD   Well, we're limited, as you know, by our moniker: Task Force Ten. Ten superheroes, not eleven.

SHARK   Oh. I never thought of that. I thought you were the tenth task force.

BRICKYARD   Yes, well . . . That's irrelevant now because we also can't have nine in Task Force Ten.

SHARK   Nine? Oh, someone's retiring?

BRICKYARD   That's not exactly the word we'd use. Well, I guess you can say they've retired. Anyway, we do need to get on with your interview. I have a funeral to attend.

SHARK   Oh, my condolences.

BRICKYARD   Yes, thank you. But this interview is really more of a formality. So if we can just—

SHARK   You mean I'm in?

BRICKYARD   Well, that's the intention. It's just a small error on your resume.

SHARK   Error? Spelling error? Oh, is it the evil villains I've battled? Did I leave off Rubik man? That guy really confuses me.

BRICKYARD   He's a hard one to figure, but no. You left off your weakness.

SHARK   Sorry, my . . . weakness?

BRICKYARD   Yes. You know: Superman's is kryptonite, mine's ball bearings.

SHARK   Ball bearings?

BRICKYARD   There's no real logic to it, I know. Anyway, if we can just add yours to your resume, that'll take care of the paperwork.

(*Pause.*)

Shark?

SHARK   I don't have a weakness?

BRICKYARD   Of course you do. Every superhero has one. It's just part of who we are. With the positive comes a counter-balancing negative.

SHARK   I see. Well, I guess I've never encountered my weakness.

BRICKYARD   Didn't you get tested?

SHARK   There's a test?

BRICKYARD   Of course there's a test. It's like an allergy test but for superheroes.

SHARK   Oh, that test.

BRICKYARD   Yes. So what was the conclusion? I'll just pen it in here.

SHARK   Nothing.

BRICKYARD   Nothing?

SHARK   Nothing.

BRICKYARD   I see. Well that is inconvenient.

SHARK Wouldn't having a weakness be inconvenient? By having a weakness our enemies can use it to conquer us and continue doing evil.

BRICKYARD Yes, that is always unfortunate when it happens. But it's also what keeps us connected to our humanity. We are reminded that no one is perfect, that there is always a flaw that we have to overcome.

(*Beat.*)

Listen, Shark, I'm sorry, but without a weakness we can't bring you on to Task Force Ten.

SHARK I can't think of a single villain that has a weakness.

BRICKYARD They all have the same weakness, their over-compensating egos. It's what drives them and ultimately leads to their downfall. All this was covered in Superhero Basic Ed, part of the licensing program.

SHARK I kind of just went through the motions on that one. I was still trying to wrap my mind around being a superhero.

BRICKYARD I see. And no one else questioned your lack of a weakness, either?

SHARK It never came up.

BRICKYARD School sure has changed. But that's all irrelevant. When or if you discover your weakness I encourage you to reapply. So, good luck?

SHARK Yeah. Thanks.

BRICKYARD Don't feel bad, Shark. You'll find your place.

(*Exit.*)

SHARK (*To self.*) But I have no weakness. What kind of superhero has a weakness? What kind doesn't? Who am I?

(*Pauses. Shrugs, takes out phone and dials.*)

Rubik man.

(*Listens.*)

You earned it, quit complaining.

(*Listens.*)

Fine, I'll get mine. Whatever, just listen for a change. Any chance you have the phone number for the League of International Villains?

(*Lights.*)

END OF PLAY

WHAT SOME GIRLS DO FOR MALL GIFT CERTIFICATES

Asher Wyndham

CHARACTERS

LARISSA: 17–18.
JULIE: Early 20s.

They wear winter clothing and boots.

TIME

Evening. It's winter.

SETTING

A changing room in a clothing store in a mall. It's not necessary to realistically create the changing room. The audience can use their imagination. Maybe use tape to outline the changing room. An acting box is okay. Some women's clothes and plastic hangers scattered around. The mirror can be the fourth wall.

———————

(*At rise:* JULIE *applies mascara on* LARISSA *who is seated shivering.*)

JULIE   Stop moving.

LARISSA   So cold in this changing room. It's like an ice fishing hut.

JULIE   Want your eye poked out? I gotta do the other eye. . . .

LARISSA   It'll seem like forever. . . .

JULIE   I told you: no longer than five minutes. Five minutes means a gift certificate with a big amount. Like fifty dollars. . . . Done.

(LARISSA *looks in the "mirror" (the fourth wall).*)

LARISSA   What if kids come in?

JULIE   This isn't a toy store. And there's no supervision back here. Just make sure you lock the door before you, y'know. Turn around, lemme do your hair.

  (LARISSA *doesn't turn around.*)

  Larissa, turn around.

(JULIE *turns* LARISSA *around and brushes her hair.*)

LARISSA   What if he kisses me?

JULIE   I told him not to. Your hair . . . It's like when you were young . . . Knots. For real.

LARISSA   Ow . . . He better not be a smelly fat comic book nerd.

JULIE   Now you're being picky. (*Reveals lipstick.*) Pucker up.

LARISSA   Did you get that on gift certificate?

JULIE   Yep. Luscious Red. Remember, leave a mark.

LARISSA   Like on the stomach, like you. Better not be furry.

JULIE   You choose where you leave yours.

LARISSA   O-kay . . . Hope he's not old with halitosis.

JULIE   No. He's in his thirties, delivers feed to farms all over the place. I'm not going to be cruel and put you with a geezer for your first time.

LARISSA   Can we just do this another day and get some Taco Bell?

JULIE   You want clown face? Keep your head steady . . . . After you're done, you can get Taco Bell and more—with your mall gift certificate.

LARISSA   . . . I just want to be Larissa. Don't you just want to be you—Julie—and not some whore!

JULIE   Listen. We can't depend on charity from churches or handouts from drivers. We gotta do what we gotta to do to get what we want. Like hygiene products, decent jeans, and good food other than cup noodles. In agreement?

LARISSA   . . . I guess so. This sucks. What next? Working at truck stops?

JULIE   No. This is temporary.

LARISSA   We're going to live in your car, forever—with the spiders!

JULIE   No, we're not.

WHAT SOME GIRLS DO FOR MALL GIFT CERTIFICATES   347

LARISSA   You can't rent an apartment with mall gift certificates.

JULIE   (*Gets text, checks it . . .*) He's in the mall. We gotta hurry. Show me your position. Do it.

(LARISSA *reluctantly gets on her knees, head low.*)

You can't give BJ with your head like that. Head up. Like this. Show me those DSLs.

LARISSA   Like in that porno your ex showed me? No. How do you really know if this guy is clean!? What if he has green dick like Shrek?

JULIE   Duhh: to be safe, you make sure he wears a condom.

(JULIE *gives* LARISSA *a condom.*)

LARISSA   Aw, thanks sis. It's flavored.

JULIE   Take your coat off.

LARISSA   (*"No":*) I'm shivering.

(JULIE *quickly unzips* LARISSA'*s winter coat.* LARISSA *is wearing an ugly Christmas sweater.* JULIE *laughs.*)

JULIE   That's the ugliest sweater on the planet.

LARISSA   Mom gave this to me on our last Christmas as a joke.

JULIE   . . . Don't bring up mom. Take it off. And don't smudge your makeup.

(LARISSA *takes off her sweater with* JULIE'*s help. And then:*)

LARISSA   Mom is looking down at us, crying.

(JULIE *breaks away from* LARISSA *or tries to keep her composure as the big sister. After a moment:*)

JULIE   We're on our own, so we gotta get our own stuff. This is the only way, for now!

LARISSA   (*On the verge of tears.*) Yeah.

JULIE   (*Starts to exit.*) I'll be in the shoe section.

LARISSA   (*Suddenly.*) How do you stop yourself from crying? How?

JULIE   I, I don't cry. Because I close my eyes and think about something else.

LARISSA   Like the way it was when mom was alive? And the house? The fireplace?

(JULIE *nods "Yes." The sisters warm up a bit just on the memory of the fireplace and the love of their mother . . . then, the cold comes back to the changing room.*)

JULIE   Remember, it's temporary. (*Fighting back tears.*) I promise. See ya, sis.

(JULIE *exits with* LARISSA*'s sweater and coat.* LARISSA *waits, shivering as if she's in an ice fishing hut on the center of a frozen lake at night. She senses the stranger approaching. His footsteps are like cracks on the lake . . . and then she gets into character. Sexy. It's painful to see.*)

LARISSA   Heyy. My name is Jenna.

END OF PLAY

WHEN IT'S OVER

Merridith Allen

CHARACTERS

JEANETTE: Andy's girlfriend, 18–20.
ANDY: Jeanette's boyfriend, 18–20.

TIME

The present.

SETTING

Jeanette's small dorm bedroom

———————

(*In bed,* JEANETTE *and* ANDY *are mostly undressed. They lay next to each other, staring at the ceiling, not talking for several moments. Finally, they slowly look at one another, then quickly, immediately, look away.*)

JEANETTE   This is silly. We've had sex before. Like, dozens of—I mean . . .

ANDY   Not like that—

JEANETTE   Nothing like that. (*Pause.*) We gotta make it not weird.

ANDY   How?

JEANETTE   OK . . . first, we get dressed.

ANDY   That's easy.

JEANETTE   Right?
(*They start to get dressed, maybe awkwardly glance at one another.*)
Andrew . . . this is over. Isn't it?

ANDY   I'm sorry.

JEANETTE   No, it's, we both . . .

(*She picks up a pair of boxers, hands them to* ANDY.)

ANDY   Those aren't mine.

(*A moment. They crack up.*)

JEANETTE   Who leaves his boxers behind?

ANDY   Right?

JEANETTE   I mean, I've left a thong or two in some mattress crevice, but—

ANDY   Which mattresses?

JEANETTE   . . . sorry. Not many. I mean—sorry.

ANDY   . . . so what do we do with those?

JEANETTE   You wanna keep them?

ANDY   What?! Like a souvenir or—

JEANETTE   Brad down the hall totally hangs up every pair of panties some girl leaves behind when—

ANDY   I'm so not doing that. Keeping a trophy, Jen? That's like, what serial killers do.

JEANETTE   OK, forget it!

ANDY   Toss them. I never want to speak of last night again. I feel it's better that way.

JEANETTE   Andy, is there . . . anything you want to tell me?

ANDY   Like what?

JEANETTE   Like . . . I dunno. Just, the way you were, last night, with Rob . . . I mean, maybe it was a little weird for us—you and me—but with him, it was kinda hot—

ANDY   Not "kinda"—I mean—

JEANETTE   Yeah. Exactly.

ANDY   Oh . . . I guess you . . . OK. Jen, you are totally my best friend, but . . .

JEANETTE   You like guys.

ANDY   Yeah. (*Pause.*) And girls. Sometimes. I mean, you. I did like you, like, I'm attracted to you, just nothing near the way I'm attracted to . . .

JEANETTE   Say, Rob? (ANDY *nods.*) OH MY GOD, I'M SO GLAD YOU TOLD ME!

(*She hugs him.*)

It's totally not all me, this weird—

ANDY   Yeah. I mean, no, not all you, no way. (Pause.) You think . . . I mean, can we . . . ?

JEANETTE   Make it not weird?

ANDY   Is that possible?

JEANETTE   I think . . . I want breakfast. And coffee. Definitely a bagel. And I think . . . we can just, sit at the deli, and talk, and . . . we can try. Maybe it won't happen today, but, we can just, be there, as best friends, and later—whenever later is—maybe it'll stop being weird and just be . . . us.

ANDY   I like the way you think.

JEANETTE   I try.

ANDY   You're really . . . I still love you. You know that, right?

JEANETTE   I still love you too. Always.

ANDY   Hey, Jen?

JEANETTE   Hmm?

ANDY   Which one of us do you think he liked better?

(*She swats him with the boxers. They laugh. Lights fade.*)

END OF PLAY

More Titles from The Applause Acting Series

How I Did It
Establishing a Playwriting Career
edited by Lawrence Harbison
9781480369634................$24.99

25 10-Minute Plays for Teens
edited by Lawrence Harbison
9781480387768................$16.99

More 10-Minute Plays for Teens
edited by Lawrence Harbison
9781495011801.................$9.99

10-Minute Plays for Kids
edited by Lawrence Harbison
9781495053399.................$9.99

On Singing Onstage
by David Craig
9781557830432................$18.99

The Stanislavsky Technique: Russia
by Mel Gordon
9780936839080................$16.95

Speak with Distinction
by Edith Skinner/Revised with New Material Added by Timothy Monich and Lilene Mansell
9781557830470................$39.99

Recycling Shakespeare
by Charles Marowitz
9781557830944................$14.95

Acting in Film
by Michael Caine
9781557832771................$19.99

The Actor and the Text
by Cicely Berry
9781557831385................$22.99

The Craftsmen of Dionysus
by Jerome Rockwood
9781557831552................$19.99

A Performer Prepares
by David Craig
9781557833952................$19.99

Directing the Action
by Charles Marowitz
9781557830722................$18.99

Acting in Restoration Comedy
by Simon Callow
9781557831194................$18.99

Shakespeare's Plays in Performance
by John Russell Brown
9781557831361................$18.99

The Shakespeare Audition
How to Get Over Your Fear, Find the Right Piece, and Have a Great Audition
by Laura Wayth
9781495010804................$16.99

OTHER ACTING TITLES AVAILABLE

The Monologue Audition
A Practical Guide for Actors
by Karen Kohlhaas
9780879102913................$22.99

The Scene Study Book
Roadmap to Success
by Bruce Miller
9780879103712................$16.99

Acting Solo
Roadmap to Success
by Bruce Miller
9780879103750................$16.99

Actor's Alchemy
Finding the Gold in the Script
by Bruce Miller
9780879103835................$16.99

Stella Adler – The Art of Acting
compiled & edited by Howard Kissel
9781557833730................$29.99

Acting with Adler
by Joanna Rotté
9780879102982................$16.99

Accents
A Manual for Actors –
Revised & Expanded Edition
by Robert Blumenfeld
9780879109677................$29.99

Acting with the Voice
The Art of Recording Books
by Robert Blumenfeld
9780879103019................$19.95

APPLAUSE
THEATRE & CINEMA BOOKS
AN IMPRINT OF
HAL•LEONARD
www.halleonardbooks.com

Monologue and Scene Books

Best Contemporary Monologues for Kids Ages 7-15
edited by
Lawrence Harbison
9781495011771 .... $16.99

Best Contemporary Monologues for Men 18-35
edited by
Lawrence Harbison
9781480369610 .... $16.99

Best Contemporary Monologues for Women 18-35
edited by
Lawrence Harbison
9781480369627 .... $16.99

Best Monologues from The Best American Short Plays, Volume Three
edited by
William W. Demastes
9781480397408 .... $19.99

Best Monologues from The Best American Short Plays, Volume Two
edited by
William W. Demastes
9781480385481 .... $19.99

Best Monologues from The Best American Short Plays, Volume One
edited by
William W. Demastes
9781480331556 .... $19.99

The Best Scenes for Kids Ages 7-15
edited by
Lawrence Harbison
9781495011795 .... $16.99

Childsplay
A Collection of Scenes and Monologues for Children
edited by Kerry Muir
9780879101886 .... $16.99

Duo!: The Best Scenes for Mature Actors
edited by Stephen Fife
9781480360204 .... $19.99

Duo!: The Best Scenes for Two for the 21st Century
edited by Joyce E. Henry, Rebecca Dunn Jaroff, and Bob Shuman
9781557837028 .... $19.99

Duo!: Best Scenes for the 90's
edited by John Horvath, Lavonne Mueller, and Jack Temchin
9781557830302 .... $18.99

In Performance: Contemporary Monologues for Teens
by JV Mercanti
9781480396616 .... $16.99

In Performance: Contemporary Monologues for Men and Women Late Teens to Twenties
by JV Mercanti
9781480331570 .... $18.99

In Performance: Contemporary Monologues for Men and Women Late Twenties to Thirties
by JV Mercanti
9781480367470 .... $16.99

Men's Comedic Monologues That Are Actually Funny
edited by Alisha Gaddis
9781480396814 .... $14.99

One on One: The Best Men's Monologues for the 21st Century
edited by Joyce E. Henry, Rebecca Dunn Jaroff, and Bob Shuman
9781557837011 .... $18.99

One on One: The Best Women's Monologues for the 21st Century
edited by Joyce E. Henry, Rebecca Dunn Jaroff, and Bob Shuman
9781557837004 .... $18.99

One on One: The Best Men's Monologues for the Nineties
edited by Jack Temchin
9781557831514 .... $12.95

One on One: The Best Women's Monologues for the Nineties
edited by Jack Temchin
9781557831521 .... $11.95

One on One: Playing with a Purpose
Monologues for Kids Ages 7-15
edited by Stephen Fife and Bob Shuman with contribuing editors Eloise Rollins-Fife and Marit Shuman
9781557838414 .... $16.99

One on One: The Best Monologues for Mature Actors
edited by Stephen Fife
9781480360198 .... $19.99

Scenes and Monologues of Spiritual Experience from the Best Contemporary Plays
edited by Roger Ellis
9731480331563 .... $19.99

Scenes and Monologues from Steinberg/ATCA New Play Award Finalists, 2008-2012
edited by Bruce Burgun
9781476868783 .... $19.99

Soliloquy!
The Shakespeare Monologues
edited by Michael Earley and Philippa Keil
9780936839783
Men's Edition $12.99
9780936839790
Women's Edition $14.95

Teen Boys' Comedic Monologues That Are Actually Funny
edited by Alisha Gaddis
9781480396791 .... $14.99

Teens Girls' Comedic Monologues That Are Actually Funny
edited by Alisha Gaddis
9781480396807 .... $14.99

Women's Comedic Monologues That Are Actually Funny
edited by Alisha Gaddis
9781480360426...... $14.99

AN IMPRINT OF
www.halleonardbooks.com